PRAISE FOR LUKE MA▯

From *"Philosophical Questions for* ▯

Here's a huge array of questions sure to brin▯ ▯e philosopher in anyone. I appreciate how the chapter/subject for each set of questions starts with an overview and then is broken up with random facts and paradoxes on the topic. The author also shares thoughts on a few of the questions in each chapter to start us off. There are many games out there involving icebreaker and general get-to-know-each-other questions, and this book could be a bunch of those games all in one place. But it also dives very deep and is quite the mind-opener.

— ROSE ANDERSON

"Philosophical Questions for Curious Minds" is a must-read for anyone interested in philosophy. The book is filled with fascinating questions and facts that have led to some truly enlightening discussions. I appreciate the way the book is structured, with each topic presented in a clear and concise manner. Overall, this is an excellent book that I would recommend to anyone looking to engage in deep, philosophical inquiry.

— HUDSON DAVID

This book is an absolute gem. The questions presented in "Philosophical Questions for Curious Minds" are not only thought-provoking but also incredibly relevant to our lives today.

— JESSE WILKINSON

100+ UNEXPLAINED MYSTERIES FOR CURIOUS MINDS

100+ UNEXPLAINED MYSTERIES FOR CURIOUS MINDS

UNRAVELING THE WORLD'S GREATEST ENIGMAS, FROM LOST CIVILIZATIONS TO CRYPTIC CREATURES, ALIEN ENCOUNTERS, TIME TRAVEL MYSTERIES, AND MORE

THE ULTIMATE 100 SERIES

LUKE MARSH

Book
Bound Studios

To the dreamers, the skeptics, the curious, and the brave, who dare to question the world around them and seek answers in the shadows of the unknown.

In the end, we will not remember the words of our enemies, but the silence of our friends.

— MARTIN LUTHER KING JR.

CONTENTS

~~$10.99~~ FREE EBOOK

Receive Your Free Copy of 100+ Interesting Real Stories

Or visit:
bookboundstudios.wixsite.com/luke-marsh

DELVING INTO THE UNKNOWN

From the dawn of human history, we have been captivated by the unexplained, the enigmatic, and the mysterious. Our innate curiosity and desire for understanding have driven us to explore the ocean's depths, the vastness of space, and the complexities of our minds. Yet, despite our relentless pursuit of knowledge, countless mysteries continue to elude us, leaving us to ponder their origins and implications.

As we stand on the precipice of the unknown, we cannot help but feel a sense of awe and wonder at the vast abyss of mystery that lies before us. This abyss has inspired countless tales, legends, and myths as we attempt to make sense of the seemingly inexplicable phenomena surrounding us. From ancient civilizations to modern-day societies, the allure of the unexplained has transcended time and culture, captivating the imaginations of generations.

In this book, we will journey into the heart of the unknown, delving into the depths of the world's most intriguing and perplexing mysteries. We will explore enigmas that have baffled scientists, historians, and researchers for centuries and attempt to shed light on the shadows that continue to obscure our understanding of these phenomena.

As we venture into the abyss of mystery, we must approach our exploration with open minds and curious spirits. We aim to uncover the truth behind these enigmatic mysteries only through curiosity and a willingness to challenge our preconceived notions. And while we may not find definitive answers to every question that arises, we will undoubtedly gain a deeper appreciation for the complexity and wonder of the world in which we live.

So, let us embark on this journey together into the unknown and seek to unravel the mysteries that have captivated our imaginations and fueled our curiosity for millennia. For it is in the pursuit of truth and understanding that we come alive, and in exploring the unexplained, we find the most profound and enduring mysteries of all.

The Allure of the Unexplained Throughout History

Since the dawn of human civilization, the allure of the unexplained has captivated the minds and hearts of countless individuals. The mysteries that have persisted throughout history, defying explanation and eluding our grasp, have constantly reminded us of the vastness of the unknown. These enigmas have shaped our collective consciousness, inspiring curiosity, wonder, and even fear in the face of the inexplicable.

The fascination with the unexplained can be traced back to ancient cultures, where myths and legends were born from the desire to make sense of the world and its many mysteries. From the ancient Egyptians' awe of the afterlife to the Greeks' reverence for the gods and their divine powers, the unexplained has long been a source of intrigue and speculation. These early civilizations sought to unravel the mysteries of the universe through storytelling, art, and science, laying the groundwork for our modern understanding of the world.

As time progressed, the allure of the unexplained continued to captivate humanity. The Middle Ages saw the rise of superstition and belief in the supernatural as people sought answers to the mysteries of life, death, and the cosmos. Tales of witches, ghosts, and otherworldly beings were woven into the fabric of society, reflecting the deep-seated fascination with the unknown.

The Age of Enlightenment brought about a shift in perspective as scientific inquiry and rational thought began to challenge the superstitions and myths of the past. Yet, even as the boundaries of human knowledge expanded, the allure of the unexplained remained strong. The mysteries that persisted, despite our best efforts to solve them, only served to fuel our curiosity and drive us to seek answers.

In the modern era, the unexplained continues to captivate our imagination. Advances in technology and science have allowed us to explore the depths of the ocean, the far reaches of space, and the complexities of the human mind. Yet, with each discovery, more questions arise, and the mysteries of the universe seem to grow ever more elusive.

The allure of the unexplained is deeply ingrained in our human nature. It is a testament to our insatiable curiosity and relentless knowledge pursuit. Throughout history, these mysteries have catalyzed progress, pushing us to question the limits of our understanding and to seek answers in the face of the unknown. As we delve into the mysteries presented in this book, we continue this age-old tradition, embarking on a journey of discovery and exploration that has captivated humanity for millennia.

Shedding Light on the Shadows of the Unknown

The human mind has always been captivated by the enigmatic and the inexplicable. Throughout history, we have been drawn to the unknown, seeking to uncover the truth behind the world's most baffling mysteries. From ancient civilizations to modern times, the allure of the unexplained has persisted, capturing our imagination and igniting our curiosity. This book aims to delve into the heart of these mysteries, shedding light on the shadows of the unknown and providing a fresh perspective on some of the most intriguing enigmas of our time.

The primary purpose of this book is to offer readers a comprehensive exploration of 100 unexplained mysteries spanning various fields such as history, science, nature, and the paranormal. By presenting a diverse range of phenomena, this book challenges conventional wisdom and encourages critical thinking, inviting readers to question the world and consider alternative explanations for the seemingly inexplicable.

In addition to thoroughly examining each mystery, this book aims to inspire readers to embark on their journey of discovery. By presenting the facts and theories surrounding each enigma, we hope to stimulate intellectual curiosity and foster a sense of wonder, encouraging readers to delve deeper into these mysteries and uncover new information that could help to unravel the truth.

Furthermore, this book serves as a testament to the enduring power of the human spirit and our relentless pursuit of knowledge. Exploring these unexplained mysteries reminds us of our innate desire to understand the world around us and our unwavering determination to seek the truth, no matter how elusive it may be.

This book celebrates the unknown, a tribute to the enigmatic, and a call to arms for all those passionate about unraveling our world's mysteries. As we journey through the pages of this book, we will venture into the abyss of mystery, shedding light on the shadows of the unknown and, perhaps, inching ever closer to the truth that lies at the heart of these enigmas.

How to Approach the Mysteries Within

As we embark on this journey through the enigmatic and perplexing, it is essential to establish a framework for approaching the mysteries. The unexplained phenomena we will explore in this book often must be clarified. Therefore, it is crucial to approach them with an open mind, a healthy dose of skepticism, and a willingness to delve into the unknown.

First and foremost, it is vital to maintain an open mind when examining these mysteries. While it is natural to have preconceived notions and beliefs, setting them aside and approaching each case with a fresh perspective is essential. Doing so allows us to consider alternative explanations and theories that may have been previously overlooked or dismissed.

At the same time, a healthy dose of skepticism is necessary when navigating the uncharted realms of the unexplained. It is crucial to question the evidence presented, scrutinize the sources of information, and consider the credibility of the claims. This critical thinking will help us separate fact from fiction and ensure we are not led astray by unfounded assumptions or sensationalized accounts.

As we study these mysteries, it is also vital to recognize the limitations of our understanding and the constraints of the evidence at hand. Often, the information available may be incomplete, inconclusive, or even contradictory. Acknowledging these limitations and resisting the temptation to jump to conclusions or accept explanations without sufficient evidence is essential.

In addition, it is essential to approach these enigmas with a sense of curiosity and wonder. The unexplained mysteries that we will explore in this book have captivated the imaginations of countless individuals throughout history, and this sense of wonder drives our pursuit of understanding. By embracing this curiosity, we can better appreciate these mysteries' complexities and nuances and their profound impact on our collective consciousness.

Lastly, it is essential to recognize that pursuing truth and understanding is ongoing. As we explore these unexplained mysteries, some questions remain unanswered or new questions arise. This should not be seen as a failure but rather as an opportunity to continue our exploration and deepen our understanding of the world around us.

By approaching the mysteries within this book with an open mind, a healthy dose of skepticism, a recognition of our limitations, a sense of curiosity, and a commitment to the ongoing pursuit of truth, we can navigate the uncharted realms of the unexplained and embark on a journey that is both enlightening and captivating. Happy reading!

1

ANCIENT ENIGMAS: UNRAVELING THE SECRETS OF LOST CIVILIZATIONS

Ancient Enigmas

T hroughout the ages, the allure of ancient mysteries has captivated the human spirit, igniting our curiosity and sparking our imagination. These enigmas, shrouded in the mists of time, have left indelible marks on the tapestry of human history, inviting us to delve deeper into the secrets of our ancestors. From the fabled city of Atlantis to the enigmatic Stonehenge, these ancient riddles beckon us to unravel their hidden truths and unlock the knowledge they hold.

The fascination with ancient mysteries stems from our innate desire to understand the world around us and our place within it. As we gaze upon the remnants of lost civilizations, we are reminded of the impermanence of our existence and the ever-changing nature of human society. These ancient enigmas serve as a testament to our ancestors' ingenuity, creativity, and resilience, who, like us, sought to make sense of their world and leave a lasting legacy for future generations.

Moreover, studying ancient mysteries allows us to appreciate the complexity and diversity of human culture. Each enigma offers a unique window into the lives, beliefs, and customs of the people who created them, providing us with valuable insights into the development of human civilization. By examining these ancient riddles, we can better understand the origins of our cultural practices and the shared human experiences that transcend time and space.

As we embark on this journey through the annals of history, we will explore some of the most intriguing and enigmatic mysteries of lost civilizations. From the depths of the ocean to the heights of the Andean mountains, we will traverse the globe in search of answers to these age-old questions. Along the way, we will encounter our ancestors' remarkable achievements and the enduring mysteries that continue to elude even the most dedicated scholars.

In this chapter, we will delve into the secrets of the lost city of Atlantis, ponder the purpose of the enigmatic Stonehenge, marvel at the mysterious Nazca Lines, and stand in awe of the Great Sphinx of Giza. We will also explore the ancient Sumerian civilization, the

Anasazi's disappearance, the Voynich Manuscript's unbreakable code, and the astonishing Antikythera Mechanism. Finally, we will visit the world's oldest temple at Gobekli Tepe and learn about the ancient astronomers of the Dogon Tribe.

As we unravel the secrets of these lost civilizations, we will be reminded of the power of human curiosity and the enduring fascination with the unknown, for it is in the pursuit of these ancient mysteries that we continue to push the boundaries of our understanding and forge new connections with the past, present, and future of our world.

The Lost City of Atlantis: Fact or Fiction?

The legend of the lost city of Atlantis has captivated the imagination of scholars, historians, and adventurers for centuries. This ancient enigma has its roots in the writings of the Greek philosopher Plato, who first mentioned the existence of a powerful and advanced civilization that mysteriously vanished in a single day and night of catastrophic earthquakes and floods. But was Atlantis a real place or merely a myth created by Plato to illustrate his philosophical ideas?

To explore this ancient enigma, let us delve into the primary source of the Atlantis legend: Plato's dialogues "Timaeus" and "Critias." In these works, Plato describes Atlantis as an island beyond the "Pillars of Hercules" (modern-day Strait of Gibraltar), larger than Asia and Libya combined. Moreover, the Atlanteans were a highly advanced civilization, possessing incredible technological and architectural achievements and a powerful navy that dominated the ancient world.

However, the Atlanteans' hubris led to their downfall. According to Plato, the gods became angry with the Atlanteans for their arrogance and greed. In a single day and night of catastrophic earthquakes and floods, the island of Atlantis sank beneath the waves, never to be seen again.

The question remains: was Atlantis a real place or merely a myth? Over the centuries, numerous theories have been proposed regarding the possible location of Atlantis, ranging from the Mediterranean to the Caribbean and even Antarctica. Some scholars argue that Atlantis was inspired by real ancient civilizations, such as the Minoans on the island of Crete, whose advanced culture and eventual decline may have influenced Plato's tale. Others suggest that Atlantis was purely a work of fiction, created by Plato as an allegory for his philosophical ideas about the dangers of hubris and the inevitable decline of powerful civilizations.

Despite the lack of concrete evidence to support the existence of Atlantis, the legend continues to fascinate and inspire. Countless books, films, and documentaries have explored the mystery of the lost city, and numerous expeditions have been launched in search of its remains. The enduring allure of Atlantis lies in its compelling combination of historical fact and myth, as well as the tantalizing possibility that a once-great civilization may still lie hidden beneath the waves, waiting to be discovered.

In conclusion, the lost city of Atlantis remains one of the most intriguing and enduring ancient enigmas. While it is impossible to say with certainty whether Atlantis was a real place or merely a myth, the legend continues to captivate the imagination and inspire new generations of scholars and adventurers to unravel its secrets. As we continue our journey through the mysteries of lost civilizations, let us remember that the quest for knowledge and understanding is a never-ending process and that the answers to some of history's greatest enigmas may still lie waiting to be discovered.

The Enigmatic Stonehenge: A Prehistoric Marvel

Nestled within the picturesque landscape of Wiltshire, England, lies one of the world's most enigmatic and awe-inspiring prehistoric monuments - Stonehenge. This ancient marvel has captured the imagination of historians, archaeologists, and tourists alike for centuries as they attempt to unravel the secrets behind its construction and purpose. Yet, despite numerous theories and extensive research, the true nature of Stonehenge remains shrouded in mystery, making it an enduring symbol of humanity's ancient past.

Stonehenge was constructed around 5,000 years ago and is a

remarkable feat of engineering and design. The monument consists of concentric circles of massive stones, some weighing as much as 25 tons. The outer circle, known as the Sarsen Circle, comprises enormous upright stones capped by horizontal lintels, while the inner circles consist of smaller bluestones arranged in various configurations.

Stonehenge's construction's sheer scale and precision are undeniably impressive, particularly considering the rudimentary tools and techniques available during the Neolithic period. In addition, the transportation of these colossal stones, some of which are believed to have been sourced from over 150 miles away, is a testament to the ingenuity and determination of our ancient ancestors.

But what was the purpose of this enigmatic monument? This question has puzzled experts for centuries, giving rise to numerous theories and speculations. Some believe that Stonehenge was a sacred site for religious ceremonies, while others propose that it was an astronomical observatory used to track celestial events such as solstices and eclipses. Yet another theory suggests that the monument served as a burial ground for the elite, as evidenced by the discovery of human remains.

One of the most compelling aspects of Stonehenge is its alignment with the sun's movements. The monument's main axis is oriented towards the sunrise during the summer solstice and the sunset during the winter solstice, suggesting that its creators possessed a sophisticated understanding of astronomy. This has led some researchers to propose that Stonehenge was an ancient calendar used to mark the passage of time and predict seasonal changes.

Despite the many theories, a definitive explanation for Stonehenge's purpose has yet to be agreed upon. This enduring enigma only adds to the monument's allure, as each discovery and hypothesis brings us closer to understanding the minds of our prehistoric ancestors. As we continue to study and appreciate this prehistoric marvel, Stonehenge remains a powerful reminder of the ingenuity, curiosity, and determination that define the human spirit.

The Nazca Lines: Peru's Mysterious Geoglyphs

Nestled in the arid plains of the Pampa Colorada in southern Peru, the Nazca Lines are one of the most enigmatic and captivating ancient mysteries. These massive geoglyphs, etched into the desert floor, have captured the imagination of archaeologists, historians, and enthusiasts alike for decades. Stretching across nearly 450 square kilometers, the Nazca Lines are a testament to the artistic and technical prowess of the ancient Nazca civilization that thrived between 200 BCE and 600 CE.

The Nazca Lines are a series of intricate designs, ranging from simple geometric shapes to complex depictions of animals, plants, and human figures. Some of the most famous geoglyphs include the hummingbird, the monkey, the spider, and the condor, each meticulously crafted with remarkable precision and scale. The largest of these designs extends over 200 meters in length, dwarfing any observer who ventures to explore these ancient wonders.

The creation of the Nazca Lines remains a subject of intense debate and speculation among experts. However, it is believed that the Nazca people removed the reddish-brown iron oxide-coated pebbles that cover the surface of the Nazca desert, revealing the light-colored earth underneath. By doing so, they meticulously crafted the lines and figures that have withstood the test of time, thanks to the region's dry and windless climate.

The purpose of the Nazca Lines is as enigmatic as their creation. Numerous theories have been proposed to explain their function, ranging from astronomical purposes to religious significance. Some researchers suggest that the lines were used as an astronomical calendar, with the geoglyphs representing constellations and celestial events. Others believe that the lines were part of a complex system of irrigation canals, while some argue that they were created as offerings to the gods or as a means of seeking water in the arid landscape.

Another intriguing theory posits that the Nazca Lines were used as ritualistic walking paths, where the Nazca people would traverse the lines as part of their religious ceremonies. This theory is supported by the discovery of pottery shards and other artifacts, suggesting they were used for ceremonial purposes.

Despite the numerous theories and extensive research, the true purpose of the Nazca Lines remains mysterious. What is clear, however, is that these enigmatic geoglyphs stand as a testament to the ingenuity and artistic vision of the ancient Nazca civilization. As we unravel the secrets of these mysterious lines, we are reminded of the enduring fascination with lost civilizations and the ancient world's enigmatic wonders.

The Great Sphinx of Giza: Guardian of Secrets

The Great Sphinx of Giza, an enigmatic symbol of ancient Egypt, has captivated the imagination of historians, archaeologists, and tourists alike for centuries. This colossal limestone statue, with the body of a lion and the head of a human, stands guard over the Giza Plateau, seemingly protecting the secrets of the ancient world. The Sphinx, measuring an impressive 73 meters (240 feet) in length and 20 meters (66 feet) in height, is an awe-inspiring testament to the architectural prowess of the ancient Egyptians. But what secrets does this majestic guardian hold?

The origin and purpose of the Great Sphinx remain shrouded in mystery. Although it is widely believed to have been built during the reign of Pharaoh Khafre (circa 2558-2532 BCE), there is no definitive evidence to support this claim. Some scholars argue that the Sphinx may be far older than previously thought, dating back to a time before the ancient Egyptian civilization as we know it. This theory is based on the observation that the Sphinx appears to have suffered significant water erosion, suggesting that it was built when the region experienced a wetter climate.

The purpose of the Great Sphinx is another enigma that continues to baffle experts. Some believe it was constructed as a divine guardian of the nearby pyramids, particularly the Pyramid of Khafre, which is believed to be the pharaoh's tomb for whom the Sphinx was named. Others speculate that the Sphinx may have served as an astronomical observation point, aligning with certain celestial bodies during specific times of the year. Yet another theory posits that the Sphinx represented the ancient Egyptian sun god, Ra, and was intended to be a place of worship.

Adding to the mystery of the Great Sphinx are the numerous legends and myths surrounding it. One such legend tells of a hidden chamber beneath the Sphinx, which is said to contain the lost knowledge of the ancient world. This theory has been fueled by discovering a series of tunnels and chambers beneath the Giza Plateau, although no direct connection to the Sphinx has been established. Despite numerous attempts to uncover the secrets of the Great Sphinx, it remains an enigmatic figure, silently guarding the secrets of a civilization long gone.

In conclusion, the Great Sphinx of Giza is a testament to the ingenuity and artistic skill of the ancient Egyptians. Its origin, purpose, and the secrets it may hold continue to fascinate and perplex scholars and enthusiasts alike. As we continue to unravel the mysteries of the ancient world, the Great Sphinx serves as a reminder of the enduring allure of lost civilizations and the enigmas they leave behind.

The Sumerian Civilization: Cradle of Knowledge

The Sumerian civilization, often regarded as the cradle of knowledge, was an ancient society that emerged in Mesopotamia, present-day Iraq, around 4500 BCE. This remarkable civilization was responsible for many groundbreaking innovations and advancements in various fields, such as agriculture, architecture, literature, and the arts. The Sumerians were also the first to develop a system of writing known as cuneiform, which paved the way for the documentation of human history and the exchange of ideas.

The Sumerian civilization was centered around a collection of city-states governed by their ruler. These city-states were often at odds, engaging in frequent conflicts and power struggles. Despite these tensions, the Sumerians established a cohesive society that thrived on trade, agriculture, and technological advancements.

One of the most significant achievements of the Sumerian civilization was developing the cuneiform writing system. This system, which utilized wedge-shaped marks on clay tablets, allowed the Sumerians to record their history, laws, and religious beliefs. The invention of writing was a monumental step forward for humanity, as it enabled the preservation of knowledge and the communication of complex ideas across vast distances.

The Sumerians were also skilled in agriculture, having developed advanced irrigation systems to cultivate the fertile lands between the Tigris and Euphrates rivers. This agricultural prowess enabled the Sumerians to support a growing population and foster the growth of their civilization.

In addition to their agricultural and literary achievements, the Sumerians were also skilled architects and engineers. They constructed monumental structures such as ziggurats, which were massive, terraced temples that served as religious and administrative centers. These impressive structures showcased the Sumerians' engineering mastery and reverence for their gods.

The Sumerian civilization was also home to a rich and diverse culture, with a pantheon of gods and goddesses, intricate mythologies, and a thriving artistic tradition. For example, the Epic of Gilgamesh, one of the earliest known works of literature, originated in Sumer and tells the story of a legendary king's quest for immortality. This epic poem, along with other Sumerian myths and legends, provides a fascinating glimpse into the beliefs and values of this ancient society.

The Sumerian civilization eventually declined around 2000 BCE, succumbing to invasions and the rise of other powerful empires in the region. However, the legacy of the Sumerians lives on through their many contributions to human knowledge and culture. Their innovations in writing, agriculture, architecture, and the arts continue to shape our world today and serve as a testament to the ingenuity and resilience of this ancient civilization. As we continue to unravel the secrets of lost civilizations like the Sumerians, we gain a deeper understanding of our shared human history and the enduring fascination with the mysteries of the past.

The Anasazi: Disappearance of the Ancient Puebloans

The Anasazi, a term derived from the Navajo language meaning "ancient enemies" or "ancient ones," were a highly advanced civilization that inhabited the Four Corners region of the United States, where the states of Arizona, Colorado, New Mexico, and Utah meet. Flourishing between 900 and 1300 CE, the Anasazi were skilled farmers, architects, and artisans, leaving a rich cultural heritage in intricate pottery, petroglyphs, and remarkable cliff dwellings.

The Anasazi are best known for their impressive architectural feats, such as the Cliff Palace at Mesa Verde and the multi-storied Pueblo Bonito in Chaco Canyon. These structures, built with incredible precision and craftsmanship, were often situated in hard-to-reach locations, providing natural defense and access to vital resources. In addition, the Anasazi's agricultural prowess allowed them to cultivate corn, beans, and squash in the harsh desert environment, sustaining a growing population and fueling their cultural expansion.

However, around the late 13th century, the Anasazi civilization began to decline, and by the early 14th century, they had vanished entirely. The sudden disappearance of the Anasazi has puzzled archaeologists and historians for centuries, with numerous theories proposed to explain their enigmatic departure.

One of the most widely accepted theories is that environmental factors, such as prolonged drought and resource depletion, forced the Anasazi to abandon their homes in search of more fertile lands. However, tree-ring data from the region indicates that the area experienced a severe drought between 1276 and 1299 CE, which would have made it difficult for the Anasazi to maintain their agricultural practices and support their population.

Another theory suggests that internal conflict and warfare may have contributed to the Anasazi's decline. Evidence of violence, such as burned villages and human remains with signs of trauma, has been discovered at some Anasazi sites. It is possible that competition for scarce resources during the drought led to increased tensions and, ultimately, the disintegration of their society.

Some researchers propose that the Anasazi did not disappear but assimilated into neighboring cultures, such as the Hopi, Zuni, and Rio Grande Pueblo tribes. Similarities in pottery styles, architecture, and religious practices between the Anasazi and these contemporary tribes support this theory. However, scholars have debated the exact nature of this assimilation and its reasons.

The disappearance of the Anasazi is a captivating mystery that intrigues researchers and enthusiasts alike. While we may never know the whole story behind their sudden departure, the remnants of their civilization serve as a testament to their ingenuity and resilience in the face of adversity. As we continue to study the Anasazi, we are reminded of the fragility of human societies and the importance of understanding our past to better navigate the challenges of the present.

The Voynich Manuscript: An Unbreakable Code

In ancient enigmas, few artifacts have captured the imagination and curiosity of scholars and enthusiasts as much as the Voynich Manuscript. Yet, this peculiar document, named after its discoverer, Wilfrid Voynich, has remained a mystery since its unearthing in 1912. The manuscript, consisting of 240 pages of vellum, is filled with cryptic text and enigmatic illustrations that have baffled experts for over a century.

The Voynich Manuscript is believed to have been written in the early 15th century, based on carbon dating and the style of its illustrations. The text comprises an unknown script, consisting of approximately 25 to 30 unique characters, which have never been seen in any other known document. The manuscript's illustrations depict various subjects, including botanical drawings, astronomical diagrams, and enigmatic human figures, often interacting with strange, unidentified objects.

Despite numerous attempts by cryptographers, linguists, and historians to decipher the manuscript's text, no one has been able to crack its code or determine its purpose. Some theories suggest that the manuscript is a work of alchemy, herbal medicine, or even an elaborate hoax. However, the lack of concrete evidence supporting these claims only adds to the manuscript's mystique.

The Voynich Manuscript's unbreakable code has led some to speculate that it may contain hidden knowledge or secrets from a lost civilization. Others believe that the manuscript's author may have been a secret society member, using the cryptic text to conceal their teachings from the uninitiated. Regardless of its origins, the Voynich Manuscript continues to captivate and intrigue those who encounter it, serving as a testament to the enduring allure of ancient mysteries.

As we explore deeper into the mysterious world of lost civilizations, the Voynich Manuscript is a prime example of the tantalizing secrets that may still be waiting to be uncovered. This unbreakable code serves as a reminder that, despite our technological advances and understanding of the past, mysteries still elude even the most brilliant minds. The Voynich Manuscript, much like the other ancient enigmas discussed in this chapter, continues to challenge and inspire us to unlock the secrets of our ancestors and the mysteries of the world around us.

The Antikythera Mechanism: A Glimpse into Ancient Technology

The Antikythera Mechanism, a fascinating and enigmatic artifact, has captured the imagination of historians, archaeologists, and engineers alike. This intricate device has been dubbed the world's first computer, discovered in 1901 amidst the wreckage of an ancient ship off the coast of the Greek island Antikythera. The mechanism, a complex assembly of gears and dials, offers a rare glimpse into the advanced technological prowess of the ancient world.

Constructed around 100 BCE, the Antikythera Mechanism is believed to have been used as an astronomical calculator. The device's sophisticated system of gears and dials could predict the positions of celestial bodies, such as the sun, moon, and planets, as well as lunar and solar eclipses. It could also track the dates of the ancient Olympic Games and other significant events. The level of precision and complexity exhibited by the mechanism was unparalleled for its time and remained unmatched for over a thousand years.

The Antikythera Mechanism is a testament to the ingenuity and innovation of ancient Greek engineers. The device's intricate design and craftsmanship suggest that the ancient Greeks deeply understood astronomy, mathematics, and mechanical engineering. The mechanism's existence challenges our preconceived notions of technological advancement in the ancient world and raises questions about the extent of scientific knowledge possessed by ancient civilizations.

Despite extensive research and analysis, many aspects of the Antikythera Mechanism remain mysterious. For example, scholars still debate the device's exact purpose, its creator, and how it came to be aboard the shipwreck. Some theories suggest that the mechanism may have been a prized possession of a wealthy individual or a valuable teaching tool to impart astronomical knowledge.

The discovery of the Antikythera Mechanism has inspired a renewed interest in studying ancient technology and has led to new techniques for examining and preserving delicate artifacts. The ongoing research into this enigmatic device continues to reveal new insights into the capabilities and accomplishments of ancient civilizations, reminding us that the past still holds many secrets waiting to be uncovered.

In conclusion, the Antikythera Mechanism is a remarkable example of the technological prowess of the ancient world. This extraordinary device challenges our understanding of the past and reminds us that ancient civilizations were far more advanced than we might have believed. As we continue to unravel the mysteries of the Antikythera Mechanism, we are gaining a deeper appreciation for our ancestors' achievements and broadening our perspective on the potential of human innovation and ingenuity.

The Gobekli Tepe: The World's Oldest Temple

Nestled in the southeastern region of modern-day Turkey lies an ancient marvel that has baffled archaeologists and historians for decades. The Gobekli Tepe, which translates to "Potbelly Hill," is a sprawling archaeological site that dates back to the Pre-Pottery Neolithic period, around 9600 BCE. This enigmatic temple complex, predating even the famed Stonehenge by over 6,000 years, is considered the world's oldest known temple. Its discovery has forced experts to reevaluate their understanding of early human civilization.

The Gobekli Tepe consists of a series of circular and oval-shaped structures adorned with massive, T-shaped limestone pillars, some weighing up to 20 tons and standing over 16 feet tall. Intricate carvings of animals, such as lions, bulls, boars, and birds, decorate these pillars, showcasing the artistic prowess of the ancient builders. The sheer size and complexity of the site have left researchers wondering how a society without metal tools, wheels, or even pottery could have constructed such an architectural feat.

One of the most intriguing aspects of Gobekli Tepe is its purpose. Unlike other ancient sites, there is no evidence of permanent habitation at Gobekli Tepe, leading experts to believe it served as a religious or ceremonial center. In addition, the presence of animal bones and stone tools suggests that the site may have been used for ritual feasting and other communal activities. Some researchers have even proposed that the temple complex was a gathering place for various hunter-gatherer groups, who came together to share knowledge and resources, and perhaps even participate in religious ceremonies.

The discovery of Gobekli Tepe has also challenged conventional theories about the development of human civilization. Previously, it was believed that agriculture and the establishment of permanent settlements were the driving forces behind the development of complex societies. However, Gobekli Tepe predates the advent of agriculture by at least 500 years, suggesting that the desire for communal worship and the construction of monumental architecture may have played a more significant role in the evolution of human societies than previously thought.

Despite extensive excavations and research, many questions about Gobekli Tepe still need to be answered. Who were the people that built this awe-inspiring temple complex, and what happened to them? How did they manage to transport and erect the massive stone pillars without the aid of modern technology? And what was the true purpose of this enigmatic site? As archaeologists continue to unravel the secrets of Gobekli Tepe, we are reminded that the ancient world still holds many mysteries waiting to be discovered and understood.

In conclusion, the Gobekli Tepe is a testament to our ancient ancestors' ingenuity and determination. This remarkable temple complex challenges our understanding of early human civilization and is a powerful reminder of the enduring allure of ancient mysteries. As we continue to explore and uncover the secrets of lost civilizations, we gain a deeper appreciation for the rich tapestry of human history and the incredible achievements of those who came before us.

The Dogon Tribe: Ancient Astronomers of Africa

Nestled in the remote cliffs of the Bandiagara Plateau in Mali, West Africa, the Dogon tribe has long captivated the world with their profound knowledge of astronomy. Despite their isolation from modern civilization, the Dogon people have demonstrated an excellent understanding of celestial bodies, which has intrigued and mystified scholars and researchers.

The Dogon's astronomical knowledge came to light in the 1930s when French anthropologists Marcel Griaule and Germaine Dieterlen conducted extensive research on the tribe. They discovered that the Dogon deeply understood the cosmos, including precise information about the star Sirius, which is invisible to the naked eye. The Dogon were aware of the existence of Sirius B, a white dwarf star orbiting Sirius A, long before its discovery by Western astronomers in the 19th century. Furthermore, the Dogon accurately described the 50-year orbital period of Sirius B around Sirius A, which was only confirmed by modern science in the 20th century.

The Dogon's knowledge extends beyond Sirius, as they also possess information about other celestial bodies, such as the planets in our solar system and their respective orbits. They clearly understand the Earth's rotation on its axis and its revolution around the sun. This advanced knowledge has led many to wonder how a tribe without access to telescopes or modern technology could have acquired such precise information about the cosmos.

Several theories have been proposed to explain the Dogon's astronomical expertise. Some researchers suggest that the Dogon may have inherited their knowledge from ancient Egyptian astronomers, as there are striking similarities between the two cultures' cosmological beliefs. Others propose that the Dogon's knowledge could have been passed down from an advanced, extraterrestrial civilization that visited Earth in the distant past. While these theories remain speculative, they highlight the enigmatic nature of the Dogon's astronomical wisdom.

The Dogon tribe's unique understanding of the cosmos is a testament to ancient civilizations' vast and mysterious knowledge. Their astronomical expertise, seemingly acquired without modern technology, challenges our understanding of the history of human knowledge and inspires us to delve deeper into the secrets of our past. As we unravel the mysteries of lost civilizations, the Dogon tribe stands as a fascinating example of the untapped potential of human intellect and the enduring allure of ancient enigmas.

The Enduring Fascination with Lost Civilizations

As we have journeyed through the enigmatic realms of ancient mysteries, it becomes evident that our fascination with lost civilizations is not merely a fleeting curiosity. Instead, it is an enduring testament to the human spirit's thirst for knowledge and understanding. These ancient enigmas, from the fabled city of Atlantis to the perplexing Voynich Manuscript, captivate our imagination and challenge our intellect as we seek to unravel the secrets of our ancestors.

The allure of these ancient mysteries lies in their ability to transport us to a time when the world was still shrouded in wonder and enigma. They remind us that our history is a rich tapestry of stories, cultures, and civilizations that have shaped human evolution. As we study the depths of these lost worlds, we are unearthing the secrets of the past and gaining valuable insights into our present and future.

Moreover, the study of lost civilizations serves as a humbling reminder of the impermanence of human achievements. The once-great empires that now lie in ruins, the advanced technologies that have been lost to the sands of time, and the profound wisdom that has vanished with the passing of generations serve as poignant reminders that our civilization, too, may one day become a distant memory.

Yet, this very impermanence makes the quest for knowledge all the more vital. As we continue to explore the mysteries of lost civilizations, we are preserving their legacy and ensuring that their wisdom and achievements are passed on to future generations. In doing so, we are honoring the indomitable spirit of human curiosity and the unending pursuit of knowledge that has driven our species forward since the dawn of time.

In conclusion, the enduring fascination with lost civilizations is a testament to our innate desire to understand our origins and unlock the secrets of the past. As we continue to delve into the enigmas of ancient worlds, we are enriching our understanding of human history and fostering a deeper appreciation for the cultural diversity and intellectual achievements that have shaped our collective story. This unyielding curiosity and passion for discovery will continue to propel us forward in our quest to unravel the mysteries of the past and chart the course of our future.

2

CRYPTIDS: THE CREATURES THAT ELUDE SCIENCE

Cryptids

Throughout history, the unknown has captivated our imaginations and fueled our curiosity. We have always been drawn to the mysteries that elude explanation, and the world of cryptids is no exception. Cryptids are creatures whose existence has been suggested but not yet scientifically proven. They are the subjects of folklore, legends, and eyewitness accounts, but despite extensive searches and investigations, they remain shrouded in mystery.

The allure of the unknown is a powerful force that drives us to explore the uncharted territories of our world and beyond. It is this same force that has led countless individuals to embark on quests to uncover the truth behind these elusive creatures. The search for cryptids is not merely a pursuit of the unbelievable; it is a testament to our innate desire to understand the world around us and push our knowledge's boundaries.

This chapter will delve into the fascinating world of cryptids, exploring some of the most famous and enigmatic creatures that have captured the public's imagination for centuries. From the towering ape-man known as Bigfoot to the mysterious water beast of Loch Ness, these cryptids have become cultural icons, inspiring fear, wonder, and endless speculation.

As we journey through the tales of these elusive beings, we will examine the evidence, the eyewitness accounts, and the scientific investigations that have attempted to shed light on their existence. We will also consider the broader implications of our fascination with cryptids, the unexplained, and what it reveals about our collective psyche and quest for knowledge.

So, let us embark on this thrilling journey into the realm of the unknown, where we will encounter the enigmatic creatures that continue to elude science and captivate our imaginations. Prepare to be intrigued, mystified, and perhaps even frightened as we observe the world of cryptids and the mysteries they represent.

Bigfoot: The Giant Ape-Man of North America

The legend of Bigfoot, also known as Sasquatch, has captivated people's imaginations across North America for centuries. This elusive creature, described as a towering, hairy, ape-like humanoid, has been the subject of countless stories, sightings, and even hoaxes. Despite the lack of concrete evidence, the fascination with Bigfoot persists, and the quest to uncover the truth behind this mysterious being continues to captivate believers and skeptics alike.

The Bigfoot legend can be traced back to the indigenous peoples of North America, who shared stories of a large, hairy, man-like creature that roamed the forests and mountains. These stories were passed down through generations, and the creature became known by various names, such as Sasquatch, which is derived from the Salish word "sásq'ets," meaning "wild man" or "hairy man."

Over the years, numerous sightings of Bigfoot have been reported throughout the United States and Canada, particularly in the Pacific Northwest. Witnesses often describe the creature as standing between 7 and 10 feet tall, covered in thick, dark hair, and possessing a strong, unpleasant odor. Some accounts even mention glowing red eyes, further adding to the creature's mystique.

In addition to eyewitness accounts, various forms of alleged evidence have been presented supporting Bigfoot's existence. This includes footprints, hair samples, and even grainy photographs and videos. However, none of this evidence has been definitively proven to be linked to an unknown, large primate.

The scientific community remains largely skeptical of the existence of Bigfoot, citing the lack of concrete evidence and the improbability of such a large, undiscovered primate species. In addition, many experts argue that the sightings and evidence can be attributed to misidentifications of known animals, such as bears, or even elaborate hoaxes.

Indeed, there have been several instances of admitted hoaxes, including the infamous 1967 Patterson-Gimlin film, which purportedly shows a female Bigfoot walking through a forest clearing. While some still believe the footage to be genuine, others have come forward claiming to have been involved in creating the film as a hoax.

Despite the skepticism and lack of definitive evidence, the search for Bigfoot continues to captivate the public's imagination. Numerous organizations and individuals are dedicated to proving the creature's existence, conducting field research, and analyzing any potential evidence. In addition, television shows, documentaries, and books continue to explore the Bigfoot phenomenon, further fueling the fascination with this enigmatic creature.

In conclusion, Bigfoot remains one of North America's most famous and enduring cryptids. The allure of the unknown, combined with the desire to uncover the truth behind the countless stories and sightings, ensures that the legend of the giant ape-man will continue to thrive in the hearts and minds of those who dare to believe in the unexplained.

The Loch Ness Monster: Scotland's Elusive Water Beast

Nestled in the picturesque Scottish Highlands, Loch Ness is a deep, dark, and mysterious body of water that has captured the imagination of millions worldwide. For centuries, tales of a strange and elusive creature lurking beneath its murky depths have persisted, earning the Loch Ness Monster a place among the most famous cryptids in the world.

The first recorded sighting of the Loch Ness Monster, affectionately known as "Nessie," dates back to the 6th century when Saint Columba, an Irish missionary, reportedly encountered a ferocious beast in the loch. However, it was in the 1930s that Nessie truly captured the public's imagination, thanks to a series of photographs and eyewitness accounts.

One of the most famous images, known as the "Surgeon's Photograph," was taken in 1934 by Dr. Robert Kenneth Wilson. This iconic picture, which appears to show a long-necked creature rising from the water, has been the subject of much debate and scrutiny. While some believe it to be genuine evidence of Nessie's existence, others have dismissed it as a clever hoax.

Over the years, numerous expeditions have been launched to find definitive proof of the Loch Ness Monster. Sonar scans, underwater cameras, and even satellite imagery have been employed in the search for Nessie, but no conclusive evidence has been found. Despite this, sightings and reports of encounters continue to this day, fueling the mystery and fascination surrounding the elusive creature.

Various theories have been proposed to explain the Loch Ness Monster phenomenon. Some suggest that Nessie could be a relic population of plesiosaurs, prehistoric marine reptiles thought to have gone extinct around 66 million years ago. Others believe that the creature could be a giant eel or sturgeon, known to inhabit deep lakes and rivers.

On the other hand, skepticism argues that the sightings can be attributed to misidentifications of common animals, floating debris, or even optical illusions caused by the loch's unique environmental conditions. They also point to the lack of concrete evidence and the inconsistencies in eyewitness accounts as reasons to doubt Nessie's existence.

Regardless of the truth behind the Loch Ness Monster, its impact on popular culture is undeniable. Nessie has become a symbol of the unexplained and has inspired countless books, documentaries, and feature films. In addition, the loch has become a major tourist destination, drawing visitors worldwide who hope to glimpse the legendary creature.

In conclusion, the Loch Ness Monster remains one of our time's most enduring and captivating unexplained mysteries. Whether it is a genuine undiscovered species, a misidentified natural phenomenon, or simply a product of human imagination, the legend of Nessie continues to capture the hearts and minds of those drawn to the unknown.

Chupacabra: The Blood-Sucking Creature of the Americas

The Chupacabra, a name derived from the Spanish words "chupar" (to suck) and "cabra" (goat), is a cryptid that has captured the imagination of people across the Americas. This fearsome creature is said to be a blood-sucking beast that preys on livestock, particularly goats, leaving behind a trail of exsanguinated carcasses in its wake. Since its first reported sighting in Puerto Rico in the mid-1990s, the legend of the

Chupacabra has spread rapidly throughout Latin America and the southern United States, becoming a cultural phenomenon and a symbol of the unexplained.

The physical description of the Chupacabra varies widely, with some witnesses describing it as a hairless, dog-like creature with a pronounced spinal ridge. In contrast, others claim it to be a reptilian or even extraterrestrial being with large, glowing eyes and sharp fangs. Despite these discrepancies, the one consistent feature in all accounts is the creature's penchant for draining the blood of its victims through small, puncture-like wounds.

As with many cryptids, the existence of the Chupacabra is a subject of much debate among scientists and enthusiasts alike. Skeptics argue that the creature is nothing more than an urban legend fueled by mass hysteria and the misidentification of common animals, such as coyotes or wild dogs afflicted with mange. This skin disease can cause hair loss and the appearance of a pronounced spine. They also point to the lack of concrete evidence, such as clear photographs or physical remains, as proof that the Chupacabra is merely a figment of the imagination.

On the other hand, believers in the Chupacabra's existence cite numerous eyewitness accounts and the gruesome nature of the livestock attacks as evidence that something unnatural is at work. Furthermore, they argue that the creature's elusive nature and ability to avoid capture indicate its intelligence and cunning, making it a worthy adversary for those who seek to uncover the truth behind this enigmatic beast.

Regardless of one's stance on the existence of the Chupacabra, there is no denying this cryptid's impact on popular culture and the collective imagination. The creature has been the subject of numerous books, documentaries, and feature films. Moreover, it continues to be a source of fascination for those drawn to the mysteries of the unknown. Yet, as with all cryptids, the Chupacabra reminds us that there are still mysteries out there waiting to be solved and that the world is not as fully understood as we might like to believe.

Mothman: The Winged Harbinger of Doom

The Mothman, a creature that has captured the imagination of many, is a cryptid described as a harbinger of doom. This enigmatic being is said to be a large, winged humanoid with glowing red eyes, striking fear into the hearts of those who encounter it. The Mothman's legend began in the small town of Point Pleasant, West Virginia, in the 1960s and has since become a symbol of the unexplained and the unknown.

The first reported sighting of the Mothman occurred on November 12, 1966, when five gravediggers working in a cemetery near Clendenin, West Virginia, claimed to have seen a large, winged figure soaring above them. A few days later, on November 15, two young couples driving through the TNT area, a former World War II munitions site near Point Pleasant, reported encountering a creature with large wings and glowing red eyes. This sighting would mark the beginning of a series of encounters with the Mothman that would continue for over a year.

As word of the Mothman sightings spread, more and more people came forward with their encounters. Some reported seeing the creature flying overhead, while others claimed to have been chased by the Mothman as they drove along deserted roads. The creature was said to be incredibly fast, able to keep up with speeding cars, and even fly alongside airplanes.

The Mothman's reputation as a harbinger of doom was solidified on December 15, 1967, when the Silver Bridge, a suspension bridge connecting Point Pleasant to Ohio, suddenly collapsed during rush hour traffic. The disaster claimed the lives of 46 people, and many locals believed that the Mothman's presence in the area was a warning of the impending tragedy.

In the years since the Silver Bridge collapse, the Mothman has become a symbol of the unexplained and the unknown. The creature has been the subject of numerous books, documentaries, and even a Hollywood film. As a result, the town of Point Pleasant has embraced its mysterious resident, hosting an annual Mothman Festival that attracts visitors from around the world.

Skeptics argue that the Mothman sightings can be explained by misidentifications of large birds, such as owls or herons, or even by mass hysteria fueled by the fear and uncertainty of the time. However, for those who believe in the existence of the Mothman, the creature remains a chilling reminder of the mysteries that still elude scientific explanation.

In conclusion, the Mothman is a cryptid that has captivated the public's imagination for decades. However, its association with tragedy and disaster has earned it a reputation as a harbinger of doom. Nevertheless, its continued presence in popular culture is a testament to our enduring fascination with the unknown. Whether the Mothman is a genuine creature or simply a product of our collective imagination, its legend continues to thrive and inspire those seeking answers to our world's unexplained mysteries.

The Jersey Devil: The Fearsome Beast of the Pine Barrens

Nestled within the dense forests of southern New Jersey lies a region steeped in mystery and folklore: the Pine Barrens. This vast expanse of wilderness is home to many legends and tales, but none are as chilling and enduring as the story of the Jersey Devil. This fearsome beast has captured the imagination of locals and visitors alike for centuries, with countless sightings and encounters reported throughout the years. But what is the truth behind this elusive creature, and why has it continued to elude scientific explanation?

The legend of the Jersey Devil dates back to the early 18th century, when a woman known as Mother Leeds, a resident of the Pine Barrens, was said to have given birth to her 13th child. As the story goes, Mother Leeds, weary from her many pregnancies, cursed her unborn child, declaring it the "Devil's child." On the night of the birth, the newborn is said to have transformed into a hideous creature with a goat's head, a kangaroo's body, and a bat's wings. The creature then attacked its mother before escaping through the chimney and disappearing into the dark recesses of the Pine Barrens.

Since that fateful night, the Jersey Devil has been blamed for various strange occurrences and unexplained phenomena. Livestock mutilations, eerie howls at night, and even mysterious footprints have all been attributed to the creature. In addition, people from all walks of life have reported sightings of the Jersey Devil, including farmers, police officers, and even prominent figures such as Joseph Bonaparte, the brother of Napoleon Bonaparte.

Despite the numerous accounts and eyewitness testimonies, the Jersey Devil has remained an enigma to the scientific community. Skeptics argue that the creature is nothing more than a product of mass hysteria fueled by the region's isolation and the human propensity for fear of the unknown. Others suggest that the sightings may be attributed to misidentifications of known animals, such as the sandhill crane or the hammerhead bat.

However, for those who believe in the existence of the Jersey Devil, the lack of concrete evidence only deepens the mystery. Some cryptozoologists, or researchers who study unknown animals, argue that the creature may be a relic from a bygone era, a prehistoric survivor that has managed to evade detection in the remote wilderness of the Pine Barrens. Others propose more supernatural explanations, suggesting that the Jersey Devil may be an interdimensional being or a manifestation of dark, malevolent forces.

Regardless of the true nature of the Jersey Devil, its enduring presence in the folklore and the collective consciousness of the Pine Barrens serves as a testament to the power of the unexplained. As long as the creature continues to elude scientific explanation, it will remain a symbol of the mysteries that lurk just beyond the boundaries of human understanding, a chilling reminder of the unknown creatures that may still dwell in the shadows of our world.

The Yeti: The Abominable Snowman of the Himalayas

Nestled within the snowy peaks and treacherous terrain of the Himalayas lies a mystery that has captivated the imaginations of explorers, mountaineers, and locals for centuries: the Yeti, also known as the Abominable Snowman. This elusive creature is said to be a massive, bipedal humanoid covered in thick fur, with an appearance somewhat akin to an ape. Sightings and stories of the Yeti have been passed down through generations, fueling a sense of wonder and curiosity about the true nature of this enigmatic beast.

The legend of the Yeti can be traced back to the ancient beliefs and folklore of the indigenous people in the Himalayan region. The Yeti, or "Meh-Teh" as it is known in the local Sherpa language, was often depicted as a powerful and fearsome creature, sometimes even considered a deity. The stories of the Yeti served as cautionary tales, warning people to stay away from the dangerous, uncharted areas of the mountains.

The Western world's fascination with the Yeti began in the early 20th century when explorers and mountaineers started venturing into the remote regions of the Himalayas. Reports of strange footprints, unusual sounds, and fleeting glimpses of a large, hairy creature began to emerge, capturing the attention of the media and the public. One of the most famous early encounters occurred in 1921 when a British mountaineering expedition led by Charles Howard-Bury discovered large footprints in the snow at 20,000 feet. The press dubbed the creature responsible for these tracks as the "Abominable Snowman," and the legend of the Yeti was firmly established in popular culture.

Throughout the 20th century, numerous expeditions were launched in search of the elusive Yeti, with varying degrees of success. Some of these expeditions uncovered intriguing evidence, such as more footprints, hair samples, and even alleged photographs of the creature. However, despite these tantalizing clues, no definitive proof of the Yeti's existence has ever been found.

Skeptics argue that the footprints attributed to the Yeti could result from natural phenomena, such as melting snow or the tracks of other animals. The hair samples and photographs have also been met with skepticism, as they have either been proven to be from other animals or are simply inconclusive.

In recent years, scientific advancements and new technologies have allowed researchers to delve deeper into the mystery of the Yeti. Genetic testing of hair samples collected from alleged Yeti sightings has led to some exciting discoveries, such as identifying a previously unknown species of bear inhabiting the Himalayan region. While this may not be the mythical Yeti of legend, it does suggest that undiscovered species may still lurk in the remote corners of the world.

Despite the lack of concrete evidence, the legend of the Yeti continues to endure. The creature has become a symbol of the unknown and the unexplained, capturing the imaginations of people around the globe. Whether the Yeti is a natural, undiscovered creature or simply a myth born from the fears and superstitions of the past, its place in the pantheon of cryptids remains secure. The Abominable Snowman of the Himalayas reminds us that there are still mysteries to be solved and that the allure of the unknown will always be a powerful force in our collective imagination.

The Kraken: The Monstrous Sea Creature of Legend

The Kraken, a monstrous sea creature of colossal proportions, has haunted the imaginations of sailors, explorers, and storytellers for centuries. This legendary behemoth is said to dwell in the deepest, darkest depths of the ocean, waiting for the opportune moment to rise to the surface and drag unsuspecting ships and their crews to a watery grave. As a result, the Kraken has become a symbol of the unknown and the terrifying power of the sea, captivating the minds of those who dare to venture into its uncharted waters.

The origins of the Kraken myth can be traced back to ancient Norse sagas and Scandinavian folklore. Described as a massive, tentacled beast with a voracious appetite, the Kraken was believed to be capable of devouring entire ships and their crews in a single, horrifying instant. Over time, the legend of the Kraken spread throughout Europe, and tales of this fearsome creature were passed down through generations of sailors and seafarers.

In the 18th and 19th centuries, the Kraken began to appear in the works of prominent naturalists and explorers, who attempted to provide scientific explanations for the creature's existence. Some speculated that the Kraken was a giant squid or octopus, while others suggested it was a prehistoric marine reptile, such as a plesiosaur or mosasaur. Despite these attempts to demystify the Kraken, the creature remained shrouded in mystery, and its true nature continued to elude the scientific community.

In modern times, the Kraken has become a popular figure in literature, film, and other forms of popular culture. From Jules Verne's "Twenty Thousand Leagues Under the Sea" to the Pirates of the Caribbean film series, the Kraken has been portrayed as a terrifying and unstoppable force of nature. These depictions have only further cemented the creature's status as one of history's most iconic and enduring cryptids.

While the existence of the Kraken remains unproven, recent discoveries in the field of marine biology have provided tantalizing clues suggesting some truth to the legends. In 2004, Japanese researchers captured the first-ever images of a live giant squid in its natural habitat, proving that these elusive creatures inhabit the ocean's depths. Additionally, the discovery of colossal squid specimens in the waters around Antarctica has provided further evidence that massive, tentacled creatures lurk beneath the waves.

In conclusion, the Kraken represents the enduring fascination with the unknown and the unexplained that lies at the heart of all cryptid legends. As long as humans continue to explore the vast, mysterious depths of the ocean, the legend of the Kraken will continue to captivate our imaginations and remind us of the awe-inspiring power of the natural world.

The Thunderbird: The Massive, Mythical Bird of Prey

The skies have long been a source of fascination and mystery for humankind. From the ancient myths of gods and goddesses to the modern-day fascination with UFOs, the heavens have always held a special place in our collective imagination. Among the many enigmatic creatures that are said to inhabit the skies, one of the most enduring and captivating is the Thunderbird.

The Thunderbird is a legendary creature in the folklore of various indigenous peoples of North America. Described as a massive bird of prey, it is said to possess incredible strength and the ability to control the elements, particularly thunder and lightning. The name "Thunderbird" is derived from the belief that the flapping of its enormous wings creates thunder, while lightning is believed to flash from its eyes.

The Thunderbird has been depicted in various forms throughout history, from the totem poles of the Pacific Northwest to the pictographs and petroglyphs of the Great Plains and the Southwest. It is often portrayed as a powerful and fearsome creature with a wingspan reaching up to 20 feet or more. Some accounts even describe the Thunderbird as having supernatural abilities, such as the power to shapeshift or to create storms at will.

Despite its mythical status, there have been numerous reported sightings of the Thunderbird throughout history. In the late 19th and early 20th centuries, newspapers across the United States published stories of encounters with gigantic birds, some of which were said to have carried off livestock or even small children. These accounts have fueled speculation that the Thunderbird may be more than just a myth and could, in fact, be a real, undiscovered species of bird.

Skeptics argue that the Thunderbird sightings can be explained by misidentifications of known species, such as the Andean condor or the California condor, which have impressive wingspans and are known to soar at great heights. Others suggest that the Thunderbird may be a case of "cultural memory," where ancient encounters with now-extinct species of large birds have been passed down through generations and incorporated into folklore.

Regardless of its true nature, the Thunderbird remains an iconic figure in unexplained mysteries. Its enduring presence in the folklore and legends of North America serves as a testament to the power of the human imagination and our enduring fascination with the unknown. As we continue to explore the skies and search for answers, the Thunderbird stands as a symbol of our quest to understand the mysteries of the natural world and the enigmatic creatures that may still elude our grasp.

The Beast of Bodmin Moor: The Mysterious Big Cat of England

Nestled in the heart of Cornwall, England, lies the enigmatic expanse of Bodmin Moor. This windswept, rugged terrain has long been the subject of local folklore and legends. Still, one mysterious creature has captured the imagination of locals and visitors: the Beast of Bodmin Moor. This elusive big cat, said to roam the moorlands, has been the subject of numerous sightings, reports, and investigations. Yet, it baffles and intrigues those seeking to uncover its true nature.

The Beast of Bodmin Moor is typically described as a large, black, or dark brown cat, similar in size and appearance to a panther or puma. Sightings of the creature date back to the 1970s, with a significant increase in reports during the 1980s and 1990s. Witnesses often recount seeing the beast stalking the moorlands, its eyes glowing in the darkness, and its chilling growls and screams echoing through the night.

Several theories have been proposed to explain the presence of this mysterious big cat on Bodmin Moor. One popular explanation is that the Beast is a descendant of exotic cats released into the wild by their owners following the introduction of the Dangerous Wild Animals Act in 1976. This legislation required individuals to obtain a license to keep certain types of exotic animals. Some speculate that those unable or unwilling to comply with the new regulations may have set their pets free.

Another theory suggests that the Beast of Bodmin Moor is a native species of big cats that has managed to evade detection and scientific classification. Proponents of this theory argue that the moor's vast, remote landscape provides the perfect habitat for a secretive and elusive predator. However, skeptics point out that the lack of physical evidence, such as carcasses or clear photographs, doubts this hypothesis.

In an attempt to solve the mystery, several official investigations have been conducted over the years. In 1995, the British government commissioned a six-month study to determine whether there was any truth to the reports of a big cat on Bodmin Moor. The investigation concluded that there was "no verifiable evidence" to support the existence of the Beast. Still, it did not rule out the possibility that exotic cats could live in the area.

Despite the inconclusive findings of these investigations, sightings, and encounters with the Beast of Bodmin Moor continue to be reported. The enduring fascination with this enigmatic creature is a testament to the allure of the unknown and the human desire to explore the mysteries that lie beyond our understanding. As long as the Beast of Bodmin Moor remains at large, it will continue to captivate the imaginations of those who dare to venture into the wilds of Cornwall, seeking a glimpse of the shadowy figure that stalks the moorlands.

The Mongolian Death Worm: The Deadly Desert Cryptid

The vast and unforgiving Gobi Desert, stretching across the borders of Mongolia and China, is home to one of the most enigmatic and feared creatures in the world of cryptozoology: the Mongolian Death Worm. Known as "olgoi-khorkhoi" in the native Mongolian language, which translates to "large intestine worm," this cryptid has been the subject of numerous legends and tales for centuries. The name itself is derived from the creature's alleged appearance, which is said to resemble a thick, blood-red worm measuring up to five feet in length.

The first recorded accounts of the Mongolian Death Worm date back to the early 20th century, when Western explorers and adventurers began venturing into the remote regions of the Gobi Desert. The creature has been described as having a smooth, tubular body with no discernible head or tail. Its skin is said to be slick and slimy, with a dark red hue that allows it to blend seamlessly with the desert sands.

Its purported arsenal of deadly abilities sets the Mongolian Death Worm apart from other cryptids. According to local folklore, the creature can kill its prey from a distance by emitting a powerful electrical discharge, much like an electric eel. Additionally, it is said to possess the ability to spit a corrosive venom, capable of dissolving flesh and bone upon contact. These lethal attributes have earned the Death Worm a fearsome reputation among the nomadic tribes of the Gobi Desert, who consider it a harbinger of death and misfortune.

Despite numerous expeditions and investigations, no concrete evidence of the Mongolian Death Worm's existence has been found. Some researchers and cryptozoologists speculate that the creature may be an undiscovered species of worm or snake adapted to the harsh desert environment. Others suggest that the Death Worm could be a type of legless lizard or even a large, venomous invertebrate.

The Mongolian Death Worm has captured the imagination of people worldwide, inspiring countless books, documentaries, and even a feature film. Its enduring appeal lies in its mysterious nature and the chilling tales of its deadly abilities. The creature serves as a reminder of the many unexplained mysteries that still exist in the world, waiting to be discovered and understood.

In conclusion, the Mongolian Death Worm remains one of the most intriguing and enigmatic cryptids in the world of unexplained mysteries. Its lethal abilities, coupled with the inhospitable environment it is said to inhabit, make it a fascinating subject for cryptozoologists and enthusiasts alike. As long as the sands of the Gobi Desert continue to shift and conceal its secrets, the legend of the Mongolian Death Worm will endure, captivating the minds of those who dare to delve into the unknown.

The Enduring Fascination with Cryptids and the Unexplained

Throughout history, humans have been captivated by the unknown, the mysterious, and the unexplained. This fascination has led to countless stories, legends, and myths about strange and elusive creatures that defy scientific explanations. Cryptids, as these creatures are known, have captured the imagination of people from all walks of life, transcending cultural and geographical boundaries. Yet, from the dense forests of North America to the remote mountains of the Himalayas, these enigmatic beings continue to elude our understanding, leaving us with more questions than answers.

One reason for our enduring fascination with cryptids is the innate human desire to explore and discover. As a species, we are driven by curiosity and the need to make sense of the world around us. Cryptids represent the ultimate challenge to our understanding of the natural world, as they seemingly defy the established rules of biology, zoology, and ecology. Pursuing these elusive creatures offers the tantalizing possibility of uncovering new species, solving age-old mysteries, and rewriting the textbooks on the natural world.

Another reason for our interest in cryptids is the allure of the unknown. In an age where technology has made the world feel smaller and more interconnected, cryptids offer a rare opportunity to delve into uncharted territory. The possibility that these creatures exist, hidden away in remote corners of the globe, ignites our sense of wonder and adventure. The search for cryptids allows us to step into the role of the explorer, venturing into the unknown in pursuit of something extraordinary.

Cryptids also tap into our love for storytelling and the power of myth. These creatures often serve as the central figures in folklore and legends, embodying the fears, hopes, and dreams of those who share their stories. From the terrifying Jersey Devil to the enigmatic Mothman, cryptids have become cultural touchstones that reflect our collective imagination. They serve as reminders of the power of storytelling and the enduring appeal of the mysterious and the unexplained.

Finally, the search for cryptids can also be seen as a reflection of our desire to connect with the natural world. In a time when urbanization and technological advancements have distanced us from nature, cryptids offer a chance to rekindle our relationship with the wild and untamed. Pursuing these creatures encourages us to venture into the great outdoors, explore new environments, and develop a deeper appreciation for the natural world and its many wonders.

In conclusion, the enduring fascination with cryptids and the unexplained can be attributed to our innate curiosity, love for storytelling, and desire to connect with the natural world. These enigmatic creatures continue to captivate our imagination, reminding us that there is still much to discover and explore in the world around us. As long as there are mysteries left unsolved and stories left untold, the allure of cryptids and the unexplained will continue to captivate the hearts and minds of people around the globe.

3

UFOS AND EXTRATERRESTRIAL ENCOUNTERS: VISITORS FROM BEYOND

UFOs and Extraterrestrial Encounters

S ince the dawn of human history, the night sky has captivated our imagination and fueled our curiosity. The vast expanse of the cosmos, with its seemingly infinite number of stars and planets, has led many to ponder the age-old question: Are we alone in the universe? This question has given rise to countless myths, legends, and stories of strange encounters with beings from other worlds. In the 20th century, these tales began to take on a new form, as reports of unidentified flying objects (UFOs) and extraterrestrial encounters captured the public's attention and sparked heated debates among scientists, government officials, and ordinary citizens alike.

The enigma of UFOs and extraterrestrial encounters is a complex and multifaceted phenomenon encompassing various topics, from ancient astronaut theories to modern-day sightings and alleged abductions. This chapter aims to provide a comprehensive overview of this fascinating subject, delving into the history of UFO sightings, the most famous and well-documented cases, the ongoing search for extraterrestrial life, and the impact of these phenomena on popular culture and our collective imagination.

As we embark on this journey through the mysterious world of UFOs and extraterrestrial encounters, it is crucial to approach the subject with an open mind and a healthy dose of skepticism. While many UFO sightings and alien encounters can be explained as natural phenomena or human-made objects, a small percentage of cases defy conventional explanations and continue to puzzle experts and enthusiasts alike. Moreover, these unexplained mysteries fuel our fascination with the possibility of visitors from beyond and keep us searching for answers to one of humanity's most enduring questions: Are we truly alone in the universe, or is there something more out there waiting to be discovered?

The Roswell Incident: A Turning Point in UFO Research

In the annals of UFO history, few events have captured the public's imagination and fueled conspiracy theories like the Roswell Incident.

This enigmatic event, which took place in the summer of 1947, marked a turning point in UFO research and forever changed how people perceive the possibility of extraterrestrial life.

On July 8, 1947, the Roswell Army Air Field (RAAF) in New Mexico issued a press release stating that they had recovered a "flying disc" from a nearby ranch. The news quickly spread, and headlines worldwide proclaimed the discovery of a crashed UFO. However, the excitement was short-lived, as the U.S. military quickly retracted the statement and claimed that the debris was merely from a weather balloon. This explanation, though, did little to quell the public's curiosity and skepticism.

Over the years, numerous witnesses have come forward with their accounts of the Roswell Incident, many of whom were military personnel stationed at the RAAF. These testimonies describe the recovery of a metallic, disc-shaped craft and the presence of small, humanoid bodies at the crash site. The military's swift response and apparent cover-up only heightened suspicions of a government conspiracy to hide the truth about extraterrestrial visitors.

The Roswell Incident became a turning point in UFO research for several reasons. Firstly, it brought the subject of UFOs and extraterrestrial life into the mainstream, sparking widespread interest and debate. The incident also led to the formation of numerous civilian UFO research organizations, such as the Mutual UFO Network (MUFON) and the Center for UFO Studies (CUFOS), which have played a crucial role in investigating and documenting UFO sightings and encounters.

Moreover, the Roswell Incident prompted the U.S. government to take the issue of UFOs more seriously. In response to the growing public interest and concern, the Air Force launched Project Blue Book in 1952, a systematic study of UFO sightings that lasted until 1969. Although the project's official conclusion stated no evidence of extraterrestrial spacecraft, many UFO researchers believe the investigation was merely a smokescreen to conceal the truth about UFOs and extraterrestrial encounters.

The Roswell Incident's enduring legacy can be seen in the countless books, documentaries, and films exploring the event and its implications. In addition, the incident has become a cultural touchstone, symbolizing the ongoing struggle between those who seek the truth about UFOs and extraterrestrial life and those who wish to keep it hidden.

In conclusion, the Roswell Incident was a watershed moment in UFO research, igniting a global fascination with the possibility of extraterrestrial visitors and inspiring generations of researchers to seek the truth. Yet, despite the passage of time and numerous official denials, the mystery surrounding the Roswell Incident remains unsolved, and the quest for answers continues to captivate the public's imagination.

The Rendlesham Forest Incident: Britain's Roswell

The Rendlesham Forest Incident, often referred to as "Britain's Roswell," is one of the most well-documented and intriguing UFO encounters in history. This extraordinary event occurred in the early hours of December 26, 1980, near the twin Royal Air Force (RAF) bases of Bentwaters and Woodbridge in Suffolk, England. The incident involved multiple military personnel, who reported witnessing strange lights and an unidentified craft in the forest over three nights. The Rendlesham Forest Incident remains a topic of fascination and debate among UFO researchers and enthusiasts alike.

The first sighting occurred on December 26, when two USAF security patrolmen stationed at RAF Woodbridge, John Burroughs, and Jim Penniston, noticed strange lights descending into the nearby Rendlesham Forest. Believing it to be a downed aircraft, they ventured into the forest to investigate. They discovered a small, triangular-shaped craft emitting a pulsating array of lights as they approached the site. Penniston later reported touching the craft, feeling a smooth, glass-like surface with strange symbols etched into it. The craft then abruptly ascended and disappeared into the night sky.

The following night, more military personnel, including Deputy Base Commander Lieutenant Colonel Charles Halt, witnessed unexplained lights in the sky and the forest. Halt led a team into the forest to investigate and recorded his observations on an audio cassette. In the recording, Halt describes the strange lights and their erratic movements. He also reported finding indentations in the ground and increased radiation levels at the site where the craft had allegedly landed the previous night.

The final night of encounters involved a group of military personnel, including Burroughs and Penniston, who returned to the forest after hearing reports of more strange lights. This time, they encountered a red, sun-like object that appeared to send beams of light down to the ground. The object then broke into several smaller, white orbs, which flew off in different directions.

The Rendlesham Forest Incident gained widespread attention and sparked numerous official and unofficial investigations. The British Ministry of Defence (MoD) initially dismissed the event as having "no defence significance" but later released a series of previously classified documents related to the case. These documents revealed that the MoD had taken the incident more seriously than initially thought, but no definitive explanation was provided.

Over the years, various theories have been proposed to explain the Rendlesham Forest Incident, ranging from secret military experiments to extraterrestrial visitation. Some skeptics have suggested that the witnesses may have been influenced by the 1980 release of the film "Close Encounters of the Third Kind" and misinterpreted natural phenomena, such as the bright lights of the nearby Orford Ness Lighthouse. However, the multiple eyewitness accounts, physical evidence, and the high credibility of the military personnel involved make the Rendlesham Forest Incident a compelling case for further study.

The Rendlesham Forest Incident remains one of history's most significant and well-documented UFO encounters. It serves as a reminder that, despite the skepticism and dismissal from some quarters, the phenomenon of UFOs and extraterrestrial encounters continues to present a genuine enigma that demands serious investigation and open-minded consideration.

The Phoenix Lights: A Mass UFO Sighting Over Arizona

The Phoenix Lights event remains one of modern history's most significant and widely witnessed UFO sightings. On the evening of March 13, 1997, thousands of residents in Phoenix, Arizona, and the surrounding areas reported seeing mysterious lights in the sky. This mass sighting not only captured the local community's attention but also sparked a renewed interest in UFO research and the possibility of extraterrestrial life.

The Phoenix Lights incident began around 7:30 PM when a man in Henderson, Nevada, reported seeing a V-shaped object with six lights on its leading edge moving slowly across the sky. Over the next couple of hours, similar reports flooded in from various locations across Arizona, describing the object as enormous, silent, and displaying a formation of lights that seemed to defy conventional aircraft design.

As the object moved southward, it was seen by thousands of people, including pilots, police officers, and military personnel. Many witnesses reported that the lights were attached to a solid, triangular, or boomerang-shaped craft. In contrast, others described the lights as separate entities, moving in a coordinated manner. The object eventually passed over Phoenix, where countless residents saw it before disappearing.

The mass sighting of the Phoenix Lights generated significant media coverage and prompted an official investigation by the US Air Force. During a training exercise, the military initially claimed that the lights were flares dropped by A-10 Warthog aircraft. However, this explanation was met with skepticism, as many witnesses insisted that the object they saw was far too large, silent, and slow-moving to be a conventional aircraft or flares.

In the years following the Phoenix Lights incident, numerous documentaries, books, and articles have been produced, exploring various theories and explanations for the event. Some researchers have suggested that the object was an experimental military aircraft, while others maintain that it was of extraterrestrial origin. Despite extensive investigations and countless witness testimonies, the true nature of the Phoenix Lights remains a mystery.

The Phoenix Lights event has impacted UFO research and the public's perception of unexplained aerial phenomena. The sheer number of witnesses, the credibility of many of those witnesses, and the lack of a definitive explanation have contributed to the enduring fascination with this case. As a result, the Phoenix Lights continue to be cited as compelling evidence for the existence of UFOs and the possibility of extraterrestrial visitation.

In conclusion, the Phoenix Lights incident serves as a powerful reminder of the enigmatic nature of UFO sightings and the ongoing quest for answers in the field of ufology. As we explore the skies and search for extraterrestrial life, the Phoenix Lights will remain a touchstone for those who believe we are not alone in the universe.

The Betty and Barney Hill Abduction

The Betty and Barney Hill Abduction is one of the most famous and well-documented alleged alien abduction cases in history. In September 1961, this extraordinary event involved a married couple from Portsmouth, New Hampshire, who claimed to have been taken aboard a UFO and examined by extraterrestrial beings. The Hill's story captured the public's imagination and laid the groundwork for future abduction narratives and research into the phenomenon.

On the night of September 19, 1961, Betty and Barney Hill were driving home from a vacation in Canada when they noticed a bright light in the sky that seemed to be following their car. Intrigued, they stopped to observe the object, which they described as a large, silent, disc-shaped craft with a row of windows. As the craft approached, the Hills experienced intense fear and decided to flee.

During their escape, the couple experienced a "missing time" period, which they could not account for approximately two hours of their journey. When they finally arrived home, they discovered their clothes were torn and dirty, and their watches had stopped working. Over the following days, Betty began to have vivid, disturbing dreams about being taken aboard the UFO and subjected to medical examinations by small, gray-skinned beings with large, slanted eyes.

Seeking answers, the Hills eventually underwent hypnosis with Dr. Benjamin Simon, a respected psychiatrist, and expert in post-traumatic stress disorder. Under hypnosis, Betty and Barney recounted remarkably similar experiences of being taken aboard the UFO, separated, and examined by the extraterrestrial beings. They described the beings as communicating telepathically and using unfamiliar instruments to perform various tests, including taking samples of their hair, skin, and bodily fluids.

The Hill's story quickly gained widespread attention, and their case became the subject of numerous books, articles, and documentaries. Their abduction account was groundbreaking, as it was the first widely publicized report of alien abduction and introduced many elements that would become common in later abduction narratives, such as missing time, telepathic communication, and invasive medical examinations.

The Betty and Barney Hill Abduction significantly impacted UFO research and the study of alien abductions. Their case prompted researchers to take the phenomenon more seriously. In addition, it led to the development of new investigative techniques, such as using hypnosis to recover memories of abduction experiences. The Hill's story also inspired other abductees to come forward with their accounts, contributing to a growing body of evidence and testimonies.

Skeptics have offered various explanations for the Hill's experience, ranging from misidentifying natural phenomena or aircraft to the influence of sleep paralysis and vivid dreams. Some have also suggested that the couple's memories were influenced by the cultural climate of the time, which was marked by a growing fascination with UFOs and the possibility of extraterrestrial life.

Despite these alternative explanations, the Betty and Barney Hill Abduction remains a seminal case in the history of UFO research and alien abduction studies. Their story continues to captivate the public's imagination and serves as a touchstone for those who believe in the existence of extraterrestrial visitors. The Hill's experience has left an indelible mark on our understanding of the UFO phenomenon. It has inspired countless individuals to seek the truth about our place in the universe and the potential for contact with otherworldly beings.

The Travis Walton Abduction

The Travis Walton Abduction is one of the most compelling and controversial cases in the history of UFO encounters and alien abductions. This extraordinary event occurred in November 1975, when Travis Walton, a young logger from Snowflake, Arizona, claimed to have been abducted by extraterrestrial beings and taken aboard their spacecraft. Walton's story, which was corroborated by multiple witnesses and subjected to rigorous investigation, has become a cornerstone of UFO research and a touchstone for those who believe in the existence of extraterrestrial life.

On the evening of November 5, 1975, Travis Walton and six of his fellow loggers were driving home from work in the Apache-Sitgreaves National Forest when they spotted a bright light in the sky. As they approached the source of the light, they saw a large, metallic, disc-shaped craft hovering above a clearing. Driven by curiosity, Walton exited the truck and approached the craft on foot. Suddenly, a beam of light shot out from the UFO, striking Walton and lifting him off the ground. Fearing for their lives, the other loggers fled, leaving Walton behind.

When the loggers returned to the site shortly after, Walton was nowhere to be found. A massive search and rescue operation was launched, but no trace of Walton could be discovered. Finally, five days later, Walton reappeared, disoriented and confused, at a gas station several miles from the abduction site. He claimed to have been taken aboard the UFO, where he encountered humanoid beings who subjected him to various medical examinations before releasing him.

The Travis Walton Abduction case gained widespread attention and sparked intense debate among UFO researchers, skeptics, and the general public. The fact that Walton's story was corroborated by multiple witnesses, who all passed polygraph tests, added credibility to his account and made it difficult to dismiss as a hoax or fabrication. Additionally, Walton's physical condition, which included weight loss and dehydration, seemed to support his claims of a prolonged abduction experience upon his return.

Over the years, the Travis Walton Abduction has been the subject of numerous books, documentaries, and even a Hollywood film, "Fire in the Sky" (1993). The case has been scrutinized by both believers and skeptics, with some suggesting alternative explanations such as hallucinations, misidentification of natural phenomena, or an elaborate hoax. However, a definitive explanation has yet to be found that can fully account for all the details of Walton's experience and the corroborating testimony of his fellow loggers.

In conclusion, the Travis Walton Abduction remains one of history's most intriguing and well-documented cases of alleged alien abduction. The case has profoundly impacted UFO research and the study of extraterrestrial encounters, inspiring countless individuals to seek the truth about our place in the universe and the possibility of contact with otherworldly beings. Walton's story continues to captivate the public's imagination and is a powerful reminder of the mystery surrounding UFOs and extraterrestrial life. As the debate over the nature of Walton's experience continues, his abduction is a testament to the complexity and enigma of the UFO phenomenon, challenging our understanding of the world and the potential existence of life beyond our planet.

The Battle of Los Angeles

The Battle of Los Angeles, also known as the Great Los Angeles Air Raid, is a fascinating and mysterious event that occurred during World War II's early days. This incident occurred on the night of February 24-25, 1942, and involved the U.S. military firing thousands of anti-aircraft rounds at an unidentified object over Los Angeles, California. The event has since become a subject of intense speculation and debate among UFO researchers, historians, and the general public, with many suggesting that the object was of extraterrestrial origin.

In the months following the attack on Pearl Harbor, the United

States was on high alert for potential enemy attacks, particularly on the West Coast. On the night of February 24, military radar detected an unidentified object approaching the coast of Los Angeles. Fearing a Japanese attack, air raid sirens were sounded, and a citywide blackout was ordered. As searchlights scanned the skies, the military began firing anti-aircraft rounds at the mysterious object, described by witnesses as a large, slow-moving, and silent craft.

The barrage of gunfire continued for several hours, with thousands of rounds fired into the night sky. Remarkably, no enemy aircraft were shot down, and the unidentified object appeared to be unharmed by the onslaught. The following morning, the military declared the incident a false alarm, attributing the object to a weather balloon or a case of "war nerves." However, this explanation did little to satisfy the public's curiosity and skepticism.

In the years since the Battle of Los Angeles, numerous theories have been proposed to explain the mysterious object and the military's response. Some historians argue that the incident resulted from a misidentified weather balloon or aircraft. In contrast, others suggest it was a deliberate disinformation campaign designed to sow confusion and panic among the enemy. However, many UFO researchers and enthusiasts believe the object was an extraterrestrial spacecraft, citing the craft's unusual appearance, silent movement, and apparent invulnerability to gunfire as evidence of advanced technology.

The Battle of Los Angeles remains an enigmatic and captivating event in the history of UFO encounters and wartime incidents. The incident has been the subject of numerous books, documentaries, and films. It continues to inspire debate and speculation among those seeking to understand the object's nature and the military's response. As the mystery of the Battle of Los Angeles endures, it serves as a powerful reminder of the enduring fascination with UFOs, the possibility of extraterrestrial life, and the complex and often uncertain nature of wartime intelligence and decision-making.

The Belgian UFO Wave

The Belgian UFO Wave is a remarkable series of UFO sightings between November 1989 and April 1990 in Belgium. This extraordinary event involved numerous reports of large, silent, low-flying black triangles with bright lights at each corner, witnessed by thousands of people, including police officers and military personnel. The sightings were also tracked by NATO radar, adding credibility to the eyewitness accounts. The Belgian UFO Wave remains one of history's most well-documented and intriguing mass UFO sightings, sparking intense debate and speculation among researchers, skeptics, and the general public.

The first major sighting of the Belgian UFO Wave occurred on November 29, 1989, when two police officers in the town of Eupen reported seeing a large, triangular object with bright white lights hovering silently above a field. Over the next few months, similar sightings were reported across Belgium. Witnesses described the objects as larger than a football field, flying at low altitudes, and capable of incredible speeds and maneuvers.

The Belgian military took the sightings seriously and launched an investigation in cooperation with civilian UFO research organizations. On several occasions, F-16 fighter jets were scrambled to intercept the mysterious objects. Still, the pilots could not make visual contact or maintain radar lock, as the UFOs seemed to evade pursuit easily. The objects were also tracked by ground-based radar stations, which recorded unexplained and seemingly impossible movements, such as sudden accelerations and sharp turns.

The Belgian UFO Wave peaked on the night of March 30-31, 1990, when a mass sighting occurred involving thousands of witnesses across Belgium. This event, known as the "Belgian Flap," prompted widespread media coverage and public interest in Belgium and worldwide. The Belgian Air Force held a press conference to address the sightings, acknowledging the objects' unexplained nature and their aircraft's inability to intercept them.

Despite numerous investigations and attempts to explain the

Belgian UFO Wave, a definitive explanation has yet to be found. Some skeptics have suggested that the sightings resulted from misidentified aircraft, such as stealth bombers or helicopters, while others have proposed natural phenomena, such as atmospheric reflections or temperature inversions. However, these explanations have been challenged by the sheer number of witnesses, the consistency of their descriptions, and the radar evidence.

In conclusion, the Belgian UFO Wave remains one of history's most compelling and well-documented mass UFO sightings. The event has significantly impacted UFO research and public perception of the phenomenon, demonstrating that UFO sightings can involve large numbers of credible witnesses and defy conventional explanations. As the mystery of the Belgian UFO Wave endures, it serves as a powerful reminder of the enigmatic nature of UFOs and the ongoing quest to understand the origins and intentions of these mysterious objects.

The Zimbabwe Ariel School Encounter

The Zimbabwe Ariel School Encounter is a remarkable and unique event in the history of UFO sightings and extraterrestrial encounters. This incident occurred on September 16, 1994, at the Ariel School in Ruwa, Zimbabwe, where over 60 schoolchildren reported seeing a UFO and interacting with extraterrestrial beings during their morning recess. The case has attracted significant attention from UFO researchers and the media, as it involves a large number of young, credible witnesses who provided consistent and detailed accounts of their extraordinary experiences.

On the morning of the encounter, the children were playing outside during recess when they noticed a shiny, disc-shaped object and several smaller crafts in the sky. According to the witnesses, one of the crafts landed nearby, and two small humanoid beings emerged from the vehicle. The beings were described as being approximately one meter tall, with slender bodies, large heads, and big, almond-shaped eyes.

The children reported that the beings approached the schoolyard and seemed to communicate with them telepathically, conveying messages about the importance of environmental protection and the future of our planet. Some of the children also experienced a sense of time distortion, as the encounter seemed to last much longer than the duration of their recess.

The Zimbabwe Ariel School Encounter quickly gained international attention, with UFO researchers and journalists traveling to the school to interview the witnesses and investigate the case. The children's accounts were remarkably consistent, and they could provide detailed drawings of the craft and the beings they encountered. In addition, many researchers have noted the sincerity and credibility of the young witnesses, who appeared to be genuinely affected by their experience.

Skeptics have offered various explanations for the Zimbabwe Ariel School Encounter, such as mass hysteria, vivid imaginations, or the influence of popular culture and media. However, these explanations have been challenged by the consistency of the children's accounts, the absence of any apparent motive for fabrication, and the fact that the children were not exposed to television or other media that could have influenced their perceptions of extraterrestrial beings.

In conclusion, the Zimbabwe Ariel School Encounter is a fascinating and compelling case in the history of UFO sightings and extraterrestrial encounters. The incident stands out due to the large number of young, credible witnesses and the consistency of their accounts, which defy easy explanations. Furthermore, the case has significantly impacted UFO research and public perception of the phenomenon, serving as a powerful reminder of the enigmatic nature of UFOs and the potential for contact with otherworldly beings.

The Tehran UFO Incident

The Tehran UFO Incident, also known as the 1976 Iran UFO Incident, is a significant and well-documented event in the history of UFO encounters. This incident took place on September 19, 1976, when Iranian Air Force fighter jets engaged in a close encounter with an unidentified flying object over the skies of Tehran, the capital city of Iran. The event involved equipment malfunctions, radar confirmations, and multiple eyewitness accounts, making it one of the most compelling cases of UFO sightings involving military personnel.

On the night of the incident, the Iranian Air Force received reports of a bright, unidentified object in the sky over Tehran. In response, an F-4 Phantom II jet was scrambled to investigate the sighting. As the jet approached the object, the pilot reported that his communication and navigation equipment began to malfunction. His weapons system also failed when the pilot attempted to engage the object with air-to-air missiles.

A second F-4 jet was then dispatched to intercept the UFO. The pilot of this jet reported seeing a bright, pulsating light that changed colors and appeared much larger than a typical aircraft. As the jet closed in on the object, the pilot observed a smaller, detached object that seemed to be heading straight for his aircraft. The pilot initiated evasive maneuvers in response, and the smaller object eventually returned to the larger UFO.

Throughout the encounter, ground-based radar stations also tracked the unidentified object, confirming the visual observations made by the pilots. After the incident, the Iranian Air Force investigated, concluding that the object could not be identified as a conventional aircraft or natural phenomenon.

The Tehran UFO Incident has been the subject of extensive analysis and debate among UFO researchers, military experts, and skeptics. Some have suggested that the object was a secret military aircraft or a misidentified natural phenomenon, such as a meteor or atmospheric plasma. However, these explanations have been challenged by the multiple eyewitness accounts, radar confirmations, and equipment malfunctions experienced by the pilots.

In conclusion, the Tehran UFO Incident remains one of the most intriguing and well-documented cases of UFO encounters involving military personnel. The event has significantly impacted UFO research and public perception of the phenomenon, demonstrating that UFO sightings can involve credible witnesses and defy conventional explanations. As the mystery of the Tehran UFO Incident endures, it serves as a powerful reminder of the enigmatic nature of UFOs and the potential for contact with unknown objects or beings in our skies.

The Kelly-Hopkinsville Encounter

The Kelly-Hopkinsville Encounter, also known as the Hopkinsville Goblins Case, is a fascinating and bizarre event in the history of UFO sightings and extraterrestrial encounters. This incident occurred on the night of August 21, 1955, in the rural community of Kelly, near Hopkinsville, Kentucky. A family reported being terrorized by small, goblin-like creatures for several hours, leading to a police investigation and widespread media coverage. The Kelly-Hopkinsville Encounter remains one of the most unusual and intriguing cases in UFO research, sparking debate and speculation among researchers, skeptics, and the general public.

On the night of the encounter, the Sutton family and their friend, Billy Ray Taylor, were gathered at the Sutton farmhouse when Taylor reported seeing a bright, shining object streak across the sky and land in a nearby field. Shortly after, the family noticed small, humanoid creatures approaching their home. The beings were described as being around 3 feet tall, with large, glowing eyes, pointed ears, and metallic, silver skin. They appeared to be floating or hovering above the ground rather than walking.

Fearing for their safety, the family armed themselves and attempted to fend off the creatures by shooting at them. However, the beings seemed unharmed by the gunfire and continued approaching the house, peering through windows and attempting to enter the home. The creatures besieged the family for several hours before they managed to escape and seek help from the local police.

When the police arrived at the scene, they found no evidence of the creatures but did note the family's genuine terror and the damage to the property caused by the gunfire. The incident quickly gained widespread attention, with newspapers and radio stations reporting on the bizarre encounter. The story became a sensation, capturing the public's imagination and fueling speculation about the nature of the creatures and their possible extraterrestrial origins.

The Kelly-Hopkinsville Encounter has been the subject of numerous investigations, books, and documentaries, with researchers and skeptics offering various explanations for the events. Some have suggested that the family was the victim of a hoax or prank, while others have proposed that the creatures were misidentified animals, such as owls or monkeys. However, these explanations have been challenged by the family's consistent accounts, the lack of any apparent motive for fabrication, and the unusual nature of the creatures described.

In conclusion, the Kelly-Hopkinsville Encounter remains one of the most peculiar and captivating cases in the history of UFO sightings and extraterrestrial encounters. The incident has significantly impacted UFO research and public perception of the phenomenon, serving as a powerful reminder of the enigmatic nature of UFOs and the potential for contact with unknown beings. As the mystery of the Kelly-Hopkinsville Encounter endures, it continues to inspire debate and fascination among those seeking to understand the strange and unexplained events in our world.

The Ongoing Mystery of UFOs and Extraterrestrial Encounters

As we reach the end of our exploration into the mysterious world of UFOs and extraterrestrial encounters, it is important to reflect on the many mysteries surrounding this fascinating subject. Despite countless sightings, investigations, and theories, we still have more questions than answers. The possibility of life beyond our planet has captured the imagination of people from all walks of life, and the search for answers has become a global pursuit.

Throughout history, humans have looked to the skies and wondered if we are alone in the universe. From ancient astronaut theories to modern-day encounters, the idea of extraterrestrial life has persisted, fueled by the numerous unexplained sightings and incidents that have taken place across the globe. The Roswell Incident, the

Rendlesham Forest Incident, and the Phoenix Lights are just a few examples of the many cases that have left researchers and enthusiasts baffled and intrigued.

The search for extraterrestrial life has not been limited to UFO sightings and encounters. Scientific endeavors such as SETI (Search for Extraterrestrial Intelligence) and the study of exoplanets have expanded our understanding of the cosmos and the potential for life beyond Earth. However, the Fermi Paradox raises a perplexing question: if the universe is teeming with life, why have we yet to find concrete evidence?

The impact of UFOs and extraterrestrial encounters on popular culture cannot be understated. From movies and television shows to books and music, the idea of life beyond our planet has captured the imagination of millions. This fascination has also led to the growth of the Disclosure Movement, which seeks to uncover government secrets and expose the truth about UFOs and extraterrestrial life.

As we look to the future of UFO research, new technologies and methods of investigation hold the promise of unlocking the secrets of these unexplained phenomena. With the recent declassification of government documents and the increasing number of credible witnesses coming forward, the quest for answers has never been more urgent.

In conclusion, the ongoing mystery of UFOs and extraterrestrial encounters serves as a reminder of the vastness of the universe and the potential for life beyond our planet. As we search for answers, it is essential to approach this subject with an open mind, a healthy dose of skepticism, and a willingness to explore the unknown. The truth may be out there, waiting to be discovered, and it is up to us to continue the pursuit of knowledge and understanding in this ever-evolving field.

4

GHOSTS AND HAUNTINGS: EXPLORING THE REALM OF THE PARANORMAL

Ghosts and Hauntings

T hroughout human history, the idea of ghosts and hauntings has captivated the minds and hearts of countless individuals. The notion that the spirits of the deceased may linger on in our world, unable to move on to the afterlife, has been a source of both fascination and fear. Ghost stories have been passed down through generations, evolving from ancient folklore to modern urban legends. The concept of hauntings has transcended cultural boundaries, with virtually every society having unique tales and beliefs surrounding the paranormal.

But what is it about ghosts and hauntings that so deeply intrigues us? Perhaps it is the innate human desire to understand the unknown, to seek answers to the mysteries that lie beyond the veil of death. The possibility of an existence beyond our mortal lives is a tempting prospect, one that has inspired countless works of art, literature, and philosophical thought. Ghosts and hauntings glimpse this other-worldly realm, offering a tantalizing hint of what may await us in the great beyond.

For some, the fascination with ghosts and hauntings is rooted in a desire for proof of the afterlife. The idea that our loved ones may continue to exist in some form after their physical bodies have perished is a comforting thought, and the notion that they may still be with us, watching over us, can provide solace in times of grief and loss. For others, the appeal lies in the thrill of the unknown, the adrenaline rush from experiencing something that defies rational explanation. Ghost stories and haunted locations have long been a staple of popular culture, with countless books, movies, and television shows dedicated to exploring the eerie and unexplained.

This chapter will observe ten ghost sightings and hauntings, including The Bell Witch, The Brown Lady of Raynham Hall, The Whaley House, and more. Ultimately, our journey will lead us to ponder the enduring mystery of ghosts and hauntings, which continues to captivate the imagination and stir the soul.

The Bell Witch (Adams, Tennessee)

The Bell Witch is one of American folklore's most famous and chilling ghost stories. The haunting occurred in the early 19th century in the small town of Adams, Tennessee, and centered around the Bell family. The evil spirit that tormented the family became known as the Bell Witch. Her legend has persisted for over two centuries, capturing the imagination of those who hear her tale.

The story of the Bell Witch began in 1817 when John Bell, a prosperous farmer, and his family started experiencing strange and inexplicable occurrences on their property. It began with unexplained knocking sounds on the doors and walls of their home, followed by the sounds of chains being dragged across the floor. It eventually escalated to physical attacks on the family members, notably John Bell and his youngest daughter, Betsy.

The spirit seemed to have a vendetta against John Bell, causing him to suffer from seizures, facial paralysis, and difficulty swallowing. On the other hand, Betsy was subjected to violent attacks, including having her hair pulled, slapped, and even being stuck with pins. The entity was also known to speak in a disembodied voice, sometimes singing, quoting scripture, or engaging in conversations with the family and visitors.

As word of the haunting spread, people from all around the region came to witness the strange events for themselves. Among the visitors was General Andrew Jackson, who would later become the seventh President of the United States. According to legend, Jackson and his men experienced the wrath of the Bell Witch firsthand, with their wagons becoming immobilized and their horses refusing to move until they left the property.

The haunting continued for several years, with the spirit's activity waxing and waning. Then, in 1820, John Bell passed away, and it is said that the Bell Witch poisoned him with a vial of mysterious liquid found near his body. After John's death, the spirit's activity decreased significantly, and eventually, the haunting ceased altogether.

The legend of the Bell Witch has been the subject of numerous books, documentaries, and even a Hollywood film. Theories about the true nature of the spirit range from a vengeful neighbor practicing witchcraft to a manifestation of poltergeist activity caused by the Bell family's intense stress and emotional turmoil. Regardless of the actual cause, the story of the Bell Witch remains one of the most enduring and terrifying tales of ghostly hauntings in American history.

The Brown Lady of Raynham Hall (Norfolk, England)

The Brown Lady of Raynham Hall is one of English folklore's most famous and enduring ghost stories. The haunting occurs in the grand Raynham Hall, a stately home in Norfolk, England. The ghostly apparition is believed to be that of Lady Dorothy Walpole, the sister of Sir Robert Walpole, who was Britain's first Prime Minister. She is often seen wearing a brown brocade dress, which has earned her the name "The Brown Lady."

Lady Dorothy Walpole was born in 1686 and married Charles Townshend, a British statesman, in 1713. Their marriage was reportedly unhappy, with Townshend being known for his violent temper. According to legend, Lady Dorothy had an affair with Lord Wharton. When her husband discovered the infidelity, he locked her away in Raynham Hall, forbidding her from seeing her children or leaving the estate. She remained a prisoner in her home until she died in 1726, officially recorded as being due to smallpox. However, rumors persisted that her husband had murdered her.

The first reported sighting of the Brown Lady occurred in 1835 during a Christmas gathering at Raynham Hall. Colonel Loftus and another guest, Lucas, claimed to have seen a ghostly figure in a brown dress with a pale, glowing face and empty eye sockets. The apparition appeared twice, each time vanishing as they approached her.

The most famous encounter with the Brown Lady occurred in 1936 when a photographer named Captain Hubert C. Provand and his assistant, Indre Shira, visited Raynham Hall to take pictures for Country Life magazine. While setting up their equipment in the main hall, Shira saw a ghostly figure descending the staircase. Provand quickly took a photograph that would become one of the most famous and widely circulated images of a ghost. The photograph shows a ghostly figure in a long dress, with a pale, glowing face, seemingly floating down the stairs.

Over the years, there have been numerous other sightings of the Brown Lady, with witnesses often reporting feelings of sadness and despair accompanying her appearance. Some believe that Lady Dorothy's spirit remains trapped within Raynham Hall, unable to find peace due to the tragic circumstances of her life and death.

The story of the Brown Lady of Raynham Hall has captivated the public's imagination for centuries, and her legend continues to be a source of fascination for those interested in the paranormal. The haunting serves as a chilling reminder of the darker side of human nature and the potential consequences of love, betrayal, and vengeance.

The Whaley House (San Diego, California)

The Whaley House, located in San Diego, California, is considered one of the most haunted houses in America. Built in 1857 by prominent businessman Thomas Whaley, the house has a long and storied history, including a courthouse, general store, theater, and even a morgue. Over the years, numerous spirits have been reported to haunt the Whaley House, with some of the most famous ghosts being those of Yankee Jim Robinson, Thomas Whaley, and his family members.

Yankee Jim Robinson was a notorious criminal convicted of attempted grand larceny in 1852. He was hanged on the property where the Whaley House would later be built. According to legend, Thomas Whaley witnessed the hanging and was aware of the property's dark history when he built his family home there. It is said that the ghost of Yankee Jim has haunted the house ever since, with visitors reporting the sound of heavy footsteps, disembodied voices, and even the sensation of being choked.

Thomas Whaley is also believed to haunt the house, along with his wife, Anna, and their children. The Whaley family experienced a great deal of tragedy during their time in the house, including the death of their young son, Thomas Jr., from scarlet fever and the suicide of their daughter, Violet, after a failed marriage. Visitors to the Whaley House have reported seeing apparitions of the family members, hearing the sounds of children playing and laughing, and even smelling the scent of Anna Whaley's perfume.

In addition to the spirits of the Whaley family and Yankee Jim, numerous other ghostly encounters have been reported at the Whaley House. For example, some visitors have claimed to see the ghost of a young girl named Annabelle Washburn, who was accidentally killed while playing near the house. Others have reported encounters with the spirit of a former tenant, Marion Reynolds, who is said to wander the halls of the house in search of her lost child.

The Whaley House has been investigated by numerous paranormal researchers and featured on several television shows and documentaries. The house is now a museum, operated by the Save Our Heritage Organisation, and is open to the public for tours. Visitors come from all over the world to experience the haunted history of the Whaley House and to catch a glimpse of the spirits that are said to still reside within its walls.

The Whaley House serves as a chilling reminder of the darker side of human history and the potential for spirits to linger long after their mortal lives have ended. The haunting tales of the Whaley House continue to captivate and intrigue those fascinated by the paranormal and the mysteries of the afterlife.

The Tower of London (London, England)

The Tower of London, a historic castle in London, England, has a long and storied history that dates back to its construction in the 11th century by William the Conqueror. Over the centuries, the Tower has served as a royal palace, a prison, a treasury, and a menagerie. With such a rich and often dark history, it is no surprise that the Tower of London is considered one of the most haunted places in England, with numerous spirits said to roam its halls and grounds.

One of the most famous ghosts associated with the Tower of

London is that of Anne Boleyn, the second wife of King Henry VIII. Anne was executed by beheading in 1536 on charges of adultery, incest, and treason, although many historians believe her enemies fabricated these charges in court. Her ghost is said to haunt the Tower, particularly the area around the Chapel of St. Peter ad Vincula, where her remains are buried. Visitors have reported seeing her headless apparition walking the grounds, sometimes carrying her severed head under her arm.

Another well-known ghostly resident of the Tower is the White Lady, believed to be the spirit of a former queen or noblewoman. She is often seen in the White Tower, the oldest part of the complex, and is known for her strong perfume scent. In addition, visitors have reported feeling suddenly overwhelmed by the smell of roses, even when no flowers are nearby.

The Princes in the Tower, Edward V and his younger brother Richard, are also said to haunt the Tower of London. The two young boys were declared illegitimate by their uncle, Richard III, and were never seen again after being sent to the Tower in 1483. It is widely believed that they were murdered on the orders of their uncle, who then took the throne for himself. The ghosts of the two princes have been seen in various parts of the Tower, often appearing as frightened children dressed in white nightgowns.

Other spirits that are said to haunt the Tower of London include the ghosts of Lady Jane Grey, who was executed at the age of 16 after a brief nine-day reign as queen, and Sir Walter Raleigh, a famous explorer who was imprisoned in the Tower for 13 years before being executed for treason. There have also been reports of ghostly guards, phantom footsteps, and even the spectral figure of a bear, which is believed to be a remnant of the Tower's time as a menagerie.

The Tower of London's haunted reputation has made it a popular destination for tourists and paranormal enthusiasts. The stories of the spirits that linger within its walls serve as a chilling reminder of the darker side of England's history and the tragic fates that befell many of its most famous residents.

The Myrtles Plantation (St. Francisville, Louisiana)

The Myrtles Plantation, located in St. Francisville, Louisiana, is often called one of America's most haunted homes. Built-in 1796 by General David Bradford, the plantation has a long and storied history that includes tales of murder, betrayal, and supernatural occurrences. Over the years, numerous spirits have been reported to haunt the Myrtles Plantation, with some of the most famous ghosts being those of a slave named Chloe and the spirits of children who died on the property.

One of the most well-known legends associated with the Myrtles Plantation is the story of Chloe, a slave who worked in the house during the early 19th century. According to the tale, Chloe was caught eavesdropping on her master, Judge Clarke Woodruff, and her ear was cut off as punishment. To exact revenge, Chloe allegedly baked a poisonous cake containing oleander leaves, intending to make the judge sick. However, her plan went awry when the judge's wife, Sara, and their two daughters ate the cake instead, resulting in their deaths. Her fellow slaves supposedly hung Chloe as punishment for her actions or to appease the enraged judge.

The ghost of Chloe is said to haunt the Myrtles Plantation, with visitors reporting sightings of a woman wearing a turban, commonly worn by slaves to cover their hair. Other paranormal occurrences attributed to Chloe include the sound of footsteps, the appearance of objects being moved, and even the sensation of being touched by an unseen presence.

In addition to Chloe, the Myrtles Plantation is also said to be haunted by the spirits of the children who died on the property. The most famous of these spirits is a young girl named Cornelia Woodruff, one of the daughters who died after eating the poisoned cake. Visitors have reported hearing the sounds of children playing and laughing and seeing the apparitions of young girls in period clothing.

Other ghostly residents of the Myrtles Plantation include the spirits of a former owner, William Winter, who was shot on the front porch and died in his wife's arms. A young Native American woman is believed to have been buried on the property. There have also been reports of a ghostly figure known as the "Lady in White," who is said to wander the grounds and watch over the house.

The Myrtles Plantation is now a bed and breakfast, allowing guests to experience its haunted history firsthand. The plantation also offers guided tours, which delve into the property's rich past and the many ghostly legends surrounding it. The Myrtles Plantation serves as a chilling reminder of the darker side of America's history and the potential for spirits to linger long after their mortal lives have ended.

The Winchester Mystery House (San Jose, California)

The Winchester Mystery House, located in San Jose, California, is a sprawling mansion with a fascinating and eerie history. Built by Sarah Winchester, the widow of gun magnate William Wirt Winchester, the house is a testament to one woman's obsession with the supernatural and her belief that she was haunted by the spirits of those killed by Winchester rifles.

Construction on the Winchester Mystery House began in 1884 and continued for nearly 38 years until Sarah Winchester died in 1922. The mansion was built without a master plan, resulting in a labyrinthine structure with over 160 rooms, including 40 bedrooms, 2 ballrooms, 47 fireplaces, and 10,000 windows. The house also features numerous architectural oddities, such as staircases that lead to nowhere, doors that open to walls, and windows that look into other rooms.

According to legend, Sarah Winchester believed she was cursed by the spirits of those killed by the rifles manufactured by her husband's company. After the deaths of her husband and infant daughter, Sarah sought the advice of a medium, who told her that she must build a house to appease the vengeful spirits and that construction must never cease, or she would face her untimely death.

Driven by this belief, Sarah Winchester used her vast fortune to continuously expand and modify the house, with construction crews working around the clock. In addition, it is said that she held nightly séances to communicate with the spirits and receive guidance on the design of the house. The maze-like layout and architectural oddities were supposedly intended to confuse and trap the evil spirits that haunted her.

After Sarah Winchester's death, the house was opened to the public as a tourist attraction, and its quirky design and eerie history quickly captured the public's imagination. Over the years, the Winchester Mystery House has been the subject of numerous books, documentaries, and even a Hollywood film. Many visitors and staff members have reported paranormal experiences within the house, including cold spots, unexplained noises, and sightings of ghostly figures.

Today, the Winchester Mystery House remains a popular destination for tourists and paranormal enthusiasts alike. The mansion offers guided tours that explore its many rooms and delve into the intriguing history of Sarah Winchester and her belief in the supernatural. In addition, the Winchester Mystery House serves as a haunting reminder of the power of grief, obsession, and the mysteries of the afterlife.

The Amityville Horror House (Amityville, New York)

The Amityville Horror House, located in Amityville, New York, is infamous for its gruesome history and alleged paranormal activity. The house gained notoriety in the 1970s after a series of terrifying events were reported by the Lutz family, who briefly lived there following a horrific family murder in the home.

The chilling history of the Amityville Horror House began on November 13, 1974, when 23-year-old Ronald DeFeo Jr. brutally murdered his parents and four siblings while they slept. DeFeo was convicted of the murders and sentenced to six consecutive life sentences. The house remained empty for over a year until George and Kathy Lutz and their three children moved into the home in December 1975.

The Lutz family's stay in the Amityville house was short-lived, as they claimed to experience a series of terrifying paranormal events during their 28 days in the residence. These events included unexplained cold spots, foul odors, swarms of flies despite the winter season, and even physical attacks by unseen forces. The family also reported seeing green slime oozing from the walls, levitating objects, and the appearance of a demonic pig-like creature with glowing red eyes.

The Lutz family's experiences in the Amityville house were chronicled in the bestselling book "The Amityville Horror" by Jay Anson, which was later adapted into a successful film franchise. The book and films sparked widespread interest in the case and ignited a debate over the authenticity of the family's claims. Some skeptics argue that the events were fabricated or exaggerated for financial gain, while others believe the Lutz family genuinely experienced paranormal activity in the home.

Since the Lutz family's departure, subsequent owners of the Amityville house have reported no paranormal activity. Many of the home's original features have been altered to make it less recognizable. However, the legend of the Amityville Horror House continues to captivate the public's imagination. It serves as a chilling reminder of the darker side of human nature and the potential for supernatural forces to invade our lives.

The Amityville Horror House remains a subject of fascination for those interested in true crime and the paranormal. The story has inspired numerous books, films, documentaries, and paranormal research investigations. Whether one believes in the supernatural events reported by the Lutz family or views them as a clever hoax, the Amityville Horror House stands as an enduring symbol of fear and the unknown.

The Sallie House (Atchison, Kansas)

The Sallie House, located in Atchison, Kansas, is a seemingly ordinary residence with a chilling history of violent poltergeist activity and ghostly encounters. Named after the spirit of a young girl named Sallie, who is believed to be one of the entities haunting the house, the Sallie House has gained a reputation as one of the most haunted locations in the United States.

The history of the Sallie House dates back to the early 20th century when it served as both a residence and a doctor's office. According to local legend, a young girl named Sallie was brought to the doctor's office with a severe case of appendicitis. In his haste to save her life, the doctor began the surgery before the anesthesia had taken full effect, causing Sallie to die in excruciating pain. Her spirit has remained in the house ever since, seeking revenge for her untimely death.

The haunting of the Sallie House gained widespread attention in the 1990s when Tony and Debra Pickman moved into the residence. The couple began to experience a series of terrifying paranormal events, including unexplained noises, objects moving independently, and even physical attacks. Tony Pickman claimed to have been scratched, burned, and even thrown across the room by an unseen force. The couple also reported seeing the apparition of a young girl, believed to be Sallie, as well as a more sinister and evil entity.

The Pickmans' experiences in the Sallie House were documented in television shows and documentaries, bringing the haunting to national attention. Paranormal investigators and researchers have since visited the house, with many reporting their encounters with the spirits. Some theories suggest that the haunting is not only the result of Sallie's spirit but also the presence of a demonic entity that feeds on the fear and negative energy within the house.

Today, the Sallie House is open for tours and paranormal investigations, allowing visitors to experience its haunted history firsthand. The house has become a popular destination for ghost hunters and those interested in the paranormal, with many seeking to uncover the truth behind the terrifying events that have taken place within its walls.

The Sallie House serves as a chilling reminder of the potential for unseen forces to invade our lives and the mystery of what lies beyond the veil of death. The haunting of the Sallie House continues to captivate and terrify those who dare to explore its dark history and the spirits that are said to still reside within its walls.

The Ancient Ram Inn (Wotton-under-Edge, England)

The Ancient Ram Inn, located in the picturesque town of Wotton-under-Edge, England, is a historic building with a chilling reputation as one of the most haunted places in the country. Dating back to the 12th century, this former inn has a long and storied history, including tales of witchcraft, murder, and supernatural occurrences. Over the years, numerous spirits have been reported to haunt the Ancient Ram Inn, including a witch who was burned at the stake, a former innkeeper, and even a demonic presence.

One of the most famous legends associated with the Ancient Ram Inn is the story of a witch who sought refuge in the building during the 16th century. According to local lore, she was discovered and burned at the stake on the inn's grounds. Her spirit is said to haunt the room where she spent her final days, now known as the "Witch's Room." Visitors have reported feeling a sinister presence in the room, witnessing objects moving on their own, and experiencing sudden drops in temperature.

In addition to the witch, the Ancient Ram Inn is also believed to be haunted by the spirit of a former innkeeper named John Humphries, who lived in the building until he died in 2017. Humphries firmly believed in the paranormal and claimed to have experienced numerous encounters with the spirits in the inn. Visitors have reported seeing his ghost wandering the halls and interacting with guests.

The Ancient Ram Inn is also said to be home to a demonic presence, believed to reside in an area of the building known as the "Bishop's Room." This evil entity is said to be responsible for a range of terrifying phenomena, including physical attacks, disembodied voices, and even full-bodied apparitions. In addition, some paranormal investigators believe that the inn may have been built on a site of ancient pagan worship, which could be the source of the dark energy that permeates the building.

Over the years, the Ancient Ram Inn has attracted the attention of numerous paranormal researchers and television shows seeking to uncover the truth behind its haunted reputation. As a result, the inn is now open for tours and paranormal investigations, allowing visitors to experience its eerie atmosphere and ghostly legends firsthand. The Ancient Ram Inn serves as a chilling reminder of the darker side of England's history and the potential for spirits to linger long after their mortal lives have ended. The haunting tales of the Ancient Ram Inn continue to captivate and terrify those fascinated by the paranormal and the mysteries of the afterlife.

The Queen Mary (Long Beach, California)

The Queen Mary, a retired ocean liner permanently docked in Long Beach, California, is a historic vessel with a fascinating history and a reputation for being one of the most haunted locations in the United States. Launched in 1936, the Queen Mary served as a luxury passenger ship, a troop transport during World War II, and eventually a floating hotel and museum. Over the years, numerous spirits have been reported to haunt the ship, including a young girl named Jackie, a crew member who was crushed to death, and the ghost of a World War II sailor.

One of the most famous ghosts associated with the Queen Mary is that of a young girl named Jackie, who is believed to have drowned in the ship's second-class swimming pool. Visitors and staff have reported hearing Jackie's laughter, splashing sounds, and even her voice calling out for her mother. The spirit of another young girl, who allegedly broke her neck while sliding down the banister in the first-class swimming pool area, is also said to haunt the ship.

Another well-known ghostly resident of the Queen Mary is a crew member named John Pedder, who was tragically crushed to death by a watertight door in the engine room during a routine drill in 1966. His spirit is said to haunt the area around the door, with visitors reporting the sound of knocking, the sensation of being touched, and even sightings of a figure in blue overalls.

The Queen Mary is also believed to be haunted by the ghost of a World War II sailor who died onboard the ship during its service as a troop transport. The sailor, nicknamed "Half-Hatch Harry," is said to haunt the ship's lower decks, with visitors reporting the sound of footsteps, the smell of cigarette smoke, and even the apparition of a man in a sailor's uniform.

In addition to these famous spirits, there have been numerous other ghostly encounters reported on the Queen Mary, including sightings of a woman in a white gown, a mysterious figure known as the "Lady in Black," and even the ghost of Winston Churchill, who traveled on the ship during World War II.

Today, the Queen Mary is a popular tourist destination, allowing visitors to explore its historic decks and experience its haunted history firsthand. In addition, the ship hosts various events, including guided ghost tours, paranormal investigations, and even an annual Halloween attraction known as "Dark Harbor."

The Queen Mary serves as a chilling reminder of the darker side of human history and the potential for spirits to linger long after their mortal lives have ended. The haunting tales of the Queen Mary continue to captivate and terrify those fascinated by the paranormal and the mysteries of the afterlife.

The Enduring Mystery of Ghosts and Hauntings

As we reach the end of our exploration into the mysterious world of ghosts and hauntings, it is evident that the fascination with the paranormal is deeply ingrained in human culture. From ancient beliefs and legends to modern-day ghost hunting and paranormal investigations, the quest to understand and explain the unexplained continues to captivate the minds of people across the globe.

Despite advancements in science and technology, the existence of ghosts and hauntings remains a topic of debate and speculation. While some argue that paranormal phenomena can be explained through natural occurrences or psychological factors, others firmly believe in the presence of spirits and entities from another realm. This enduring mystery keeps the subject of ghosts and hauntings alive and thriving in popular culture, as evidenced by the countless movies, books, and TV shows that delve into the supernatural.

The various hauntings, from residual to intelligent and poltergeists, further add to the complexity of the paranormal world. Each haunting presents unique characteristics and challenges, making it difficult to establish a one-size-fits-all explanation for these phenomena. However, the personal stories and experiences shared by those who have encountered ghosts and hauntings serve as a testament to the profound impact that these events can have on individuals and communities.

The role of ghost hunters and paranormal investigators in this realm is both intriguing and controversial. While some view their work as a valuable contribution to understanding the unknown, others criticize their methods as exploitative or sensationalist. The ethics of ghost hunting, therefore, remains an essential consideration in the ongoing pursuit of paranormal knowledge.

In the end, the realm of ghosts and hauntings continues to be a source of fascination, fear, and wonder for many. Whether one believes in the existence of spirits or not, the stories and experiences shared by countless individuals throughout history serve as a reminder of the enduring mystery surrounding the paranormal. As we search for answers and understanding, the mysterious world of ghosts and hauntings will remain captivating for generations to come.

5

MYSTERIOUS DISAPPEARANCES: VANISHING WITHOUT A TRACE

Mysterious Disappearances

Throughout history, there have been countless instances of people, ships, planes, and even entire communities vanishing without a trace. These unexplained disappearances have captured the public's imagination, sparking endless speculation, theories, and debates. Unfortunately, in some cases, these mysteries have remained unsolved for centuries, leaving behind a legacy of intrigue and fascination.

The enigma of unexplained disappearances is a testament to the human desire for answers and understanding. We are naturally drawn to the unknown, seeking to unravel the mysteries that elude explanation. In this quest for knowledge, we are often confronted with the limits of our understanding and the vastness of the world around us. This sense of wonder and curiosity drives us to explore the stories of those who have vanished without a trace.

This chapter will delve into ten of the most captivating unexplained disappearances in history. These cases represent various circumstances and periods, from the lost colony of Roanoke to the modern-day aviation enigma of Flight MH370. Each story is unique, yet they all share a common thread: the inexplicable nature of their disappearance.

As we journey through these tales of mystery, we will encounter ghost ships, vanished aviators, and eerie geographical locations. We will examine the evidence, consider the theories, and attempt to piece together the puzzle of these mysterious vanishings. In doing so, we will explore the stories themselves and the broader implications of these unexplained disappearances on our understanding of the world.

Ultimately, the enduring fascination with vanishing acts reflects our collective curiosity and desire to make sense of the seemingly inexplicable. While we may never find definitive answers to these mysteries, the process of investigation and speculation can be just as compelling as the stories themselves. So, let us embark on this journey into the unknown and delve into the enigma of unexplained disappearances.

The Lost Colony of Roanoke: America's First Unsolved Mystery

The enigmatic tale of the Lost Colony of Roanoke has captivated historians, researchers, and the general public for centuries. As America's first mystery, it serves as a chilling reminder of the perils faced by early settlers in the New World. The story of Roanoke is one of hope, despair, and an enduring enigma that continues to baffle even the most seasoned experts.

In 1587, a group of 115 English settlers, led by Governor John White, arrived on Roanoke Island, located off the coast of present-day North Carolina. They were part of an ambitious plan to establish a permanent English colony in the New World, backed by Sir Walter Raleigh. The settlers, including men, women, and children, began to build new lives in this unfamiliar land, unaware of the fate awaiting them.

Governor White soon realized that the colony was in dire need of supplies and support to survive. He made the difficult decision to return to England, leaving behind his family and fellow settlers, promising to return as soon as possible. However, due to a series of unfortunate events, including the outbreak of war between England and Spain, White's return to Roanoke was delayed by three long years.

When White finally managed to return to Roanoke in 1590, he was met with a chilling sight: the entire colony had vanished without a trace. The only clue left behind was the word "CROATOAN" carved into a wooden post and the letters "CRO" etched onto a nearby tree. White was devastated, and the search for the missing settlers began.

Over the years, numerous theories have been proposed to explain the fate of the Lost Colony of Roanoke. Some believe that the settlers were assimilated into nearby Native American tribes, while others suggest that they fell victim to disease, famine, or hostile encounters with the indigenous population. More outlandish theories include the idea that aliens abducted the colonists or fell victim to supernatural forces.

Despite extensive archaeological investigations and historical research, concrete evidence has yet to be found to definitively explain the disappearance of the Roanoke settlers. Nevertheless, theories continue to be debated, and discoveries occasionally reignite interest in this centuries-old mystery. The Lost Colony of Roanoke serves as a haunting reminder of the challenges faced by early settlers in the New World. Moreover, it is a testament to the enduring human fascination with the unexplained.

The Mary Celeste: A Ghost Ship with No Crew

The Mary Celeste is perhaps one of the most famous and enduring maritime mysteries of all time. This enigmatic ghost ship has captured the imagination of countless generations, as the circumstances surrounding its discovery continue to baffle experts and enthusiasts alike. In this section, we will delve into the chilling tale of the Mary Celeste, a vessel found adrift and abandoned, with no trace of its crew or any indication of what could have caused their sudden disappearance.

On November 7, 1872, the Mary Celeste set sail from New York Harbor, bound for Genoa, Italy. The ship was captained by Benjamin Briggs, an experienced seafarer, accompanied by his wife, young daughter, and a crew of seven. The cargo on board consisted of 1,701 barrels of commercial alcohol intended for fortifying wine. The voyage was expected to be relatively routine, but fate had other plans.

Less than a month later, on December 4, 1872, the British brigantine Dei Gratia stumbled upon the Mary Celeste adrift in the Atlantic Ocean, approximately 400 miles east of the Azores. The crew of the Dei Gratia, led by Captain David Morehouse, was astonished to find the ship deserted, with no signs of struggle or damage. The Mary Celeste's lifeboat was missing, but the ship was still seaworthy, and its cargo remained intact. Unfortunately, last updated on November 24, the ship's logbook offered no clues about the crew's fate.

The discovery of the Mary Celeste sparked a frenzy of speculation and theories as people struggled to comprehend the circumstances that led to the crew's disappearance. Some suggested that the crew had been victims of piracy or a mutiny, but the lack of any signs of violence on board made these theories unlikely. Others posited that the crew had abandoned the ship due to perceived danger, such as an explosion caused by the alcohol fumes. However, the fact that the cargo was found undisturbed and the ship was still in good condition also cast doubt on this theory.

Another popular theory was that a rogue wave or a sudden storm had swept away the crew. This, too, seemed improbable, given the ship's undamaged state and the absence of any records of severe weather in the area. Some even ventured into the supernatural realm, suggesting that the crew had been abducted by extraterrestrial beings or fallen victim to the legendary sea monster, the Kraken.

Despite numerous investigations and inquiries, both at the time and in the years that followed, the fate of the Mary Celeste's crew remains an enigma. The ship continued to sail under different owners and names until it was deliberately wrecked in 1885 as part of an insurance fraud scheme. However, the ghostly image of the abandoned vessel, drifting aimlessly on the open sea, continues to haunt the annals of maritime history, serving as a chilling reminder of the unfathomable mysteries that still lurk beneath the waves.

Amelia Earhart: The Disappearance of an Aviation Pioneer

Amelia Earhart, a name synonymous with courage, determination, and the spirit of adventure remains one of the most enigmatic figures in the annals of unexplained mysteries. As the first woman to fly solo across the Atlantic Ocean, Earhart's groundbreaking achievements in the aviation field earned her international acclaim and inspired generations of female pilots. However, her sudden and baffling disappearance during an ambitious attempt to circumnavigate the globe would forever etch her name in the annals of unsolved mysteries.

On July 2, 1937, Earhart and her navigator, Fred Noonan, embarked on the most challenging leg of their journey – a 2,556-mile flight from Lae, New Guinea, to Howland Island, a speck of land in the vast expanse of the Pacific Ocean. Unfortunately, despite meticulous preparations and state-of-the-art navigation equipment, the duo never arrived at their destination, seemingly vanishing without a trace.

The extensive search and rescue operation that followed, led by the United States Coast Guard and Navy, proved fruitless, as no wreckage or debris from Earhart's Lockheed Electra aircraft was ever found. The official conclusion was that the plane had run out of fuel and crashed into the ocean. Still, this explanation left many questions unanswered and sparked many alternative theories.

One such theory suggests that Earhart and Noonan, unable to locate Howland Island, may have landed on the uninhabited Gardner Island (now known as Nikumaroro). Proponents of this hypothesis point to the discovery of a woman's shoe, a sextant box, and human bones on the island in the years following the disappearance. However, despite numerous expeditions to the island and extensive forensic analysis, no definitive evidence has been found to confirm this theory.

Another popular theory posits that the Japanese captured Earhart and Noonan, who believed them to be American spies. This theory is fueled by anecdotal accounts from Pacific islanders who claimed to have seen the pair in Japanese custody and alleged photographs of Earhart and Noonan in captivity. However, these claims have been debunked mainly by experts, and no concrete evidence has been produced to support the notion of Japanese involvement in their disappearance.

As the years have passed, the mystery of Amelia Earhart's disappearance has only deepened, with countless books, documentaries, and investigations attempting to unravel the enigma. While we may never know the true fate of this pioneering aviator and her trusted navigator, their enduring legacy continues to captivate and inspire, serving as a poignant reminder of the indomitable human spirit and the allure of the unknown.

The Bermuda Triangle: A Vortex of Vanishing Vessels and Aircraft

The Bermuda Triangle, also known as the Devil's Triangle, is an area of the Atlantic Ocean that has long been shrouded in mystery and intrigue. This enigmatic region, roughly bounded by the coast of Florida, Bermuda, and Puerto Rico, has been the site of numerous unexplained disappearances of ships and aircraft over the years. The stories of these vanishing vessels and planes have captivated the public's imagination, leading to countless theories and speculations about the cause of these strange occurrences.

One of the most famous incidents in the Bermuda Triangle is the disappearance of Flight 19, a group of five US Navy torpedo bombers that vanished during a routine training mission in 1945. Despite an extensive search and rescue operation, the aircraft and its 14 crew members were never found. Adding to the mystery, a search plane with a crew of 13 also disappeared while looking for the missing bombers. Unfortunately, no wreckage or debris from the bombers or the search plane has ever been recovered, fueling speculation about the supernatural forces in the Bermuda Triangle.

Another notable case is the disappearance of the USS Cyclops, a US Navy cargo ship that vanished in the Bermuda Triangle in 1918. The ship, carrying over 300 crew members and a cargo of manganese ore, was en route from Brazil to Baltimore when it disappeared without a trace. No distress signals were received, and no wreckage or debris from the ship has ever been found. The fate of the USS Cyclops remains one of the greatest maritime mysteries in history.

Many theories have been proposed to explain the strange phenomena associated with the Bermuda Triangle, ranging from the plausible to the downright bizarre. For example, some researchers have suggested that the area is prone to sudden, violent storms that can quickly engulf ships and planes. In contrast, others have pointed to the presence of large methane gas deposits on the ocean floor, which could cause ships to sink and disrupt the navigation systems of aircraft. More outlandish theories include the presence of extraterrestrial beings, time warps, and even the lost city of Atlantis.

Despite the numerous theories and speculations, no definitive explanation for the mysterious disappearances in the Bermuda Triangle has been found. While some researchers argue that the area is no more dangerous than any other part of the ocean, the enduring fascination with the Bermuda Triangle and its enigmatic history ensures that it will continue to be a source of intrigue and wonder for years to come. As we probe deeper into the mysteries of the Bermuda Triangle, we are reminded of our planet's vast, unexplored depths and the countless secrets that still lie beneath the waves.

The Dyatlov Pass Incident: A Chilling Tale of Missing Hikers

In the heart of Russia's Ural Mountains lies a chilling mystery that has haunted investigators and sparked countless theories for over six decades. The Dyatlov Pass Incident, named after the leader of the ill-fated expedition, Igor Dyatlov, is a perplexing tale of nine experienced hikers who vanished in February 1959. Their subsequent discovery, under bizarre and inexplicable circumstances, has left experts and enthusiasts searching for answers to this day.

The group, consisting of seven men and two women, embarked on a challenging trek through the remote and unforgiving terrain of the Ural Mountains. Their goal was to reach the summit of Mount Otorten, a feat that would earn them the prestigious "Grade III" hiking certification. However, as the days passed and no word came from the hikers, concern grew among their friends and families. It wasn't until February 26, nearly a month after their departure, that a search party discovered the first unsettling clues to their fate.

The hikers' tent, found abandoned and partially buried in snow, had been slashed open from the inside. Stranger still, their belongings, including warm clothing and boots, had been left behind, as if the group had fled suddenly. The search party followed a trail of footprints, some barefoot or in socks, leading away from the tent. The tracks led to the gruesome discovery of five hikers' bodies scattered across the mountainside and dressed in little more than their undergarments.

The remaining four bodies were not found until months later, buried beneath several feet of snow in a nearby ravine. These hikers appeared to have suffered severe internal injuries akin to those caused by a car crash, yet there were no external signs of trauma. One of the women was found missing her tongue and eyes, further deepening the mystery.

Numerous theories have been proposed to explain the Dyatlov Pass

Incident, ranging from the plausible to the outlandish. Some suggest that the group was caught in an avalanche, forcing them to cut their way out of the tent and flee in terror, only to succumb to the harsh elements. Others propose that they encountered a hostile military presence or stumbled upon a secret government experiment gone awry. More fanciful explanations involve extraterrestrial encounters or the wrath of the indigenous Mansi people, who believed the mountain to be sacred.

Despite extensive investigations and the passage of time, the Dyatlov Pass Incident remains one of history's most enigmatic and chilling unexplained disappearances. The tragic fate of these nine hikers serves as a stark reminder of the unfathomable mysteries that continue to defy explanation and capture our collective imagination.

Flight MH370: The Modern-Day Aviation Enigma

The disappearance of Malaysia Airlines Flight MH370 on March 8, 2014, remains one of the most baffling aviation mysteries of the 21st century. The Boeing 777 aircraft, carrying 239 passengers and crew members, vanished without a trace during a routine flight from Kuala Lumpur to Beijing. Despite extensive search efforts and numerous theories, the fate of the aircraft and its occupants remains mysterious.

The flight took off from Kuala Lumpur International Airport at 12:41 a.m. local time, with no indication of any issues. However, less than an hour into the flight, the aircraft's transponder stopped transmitting, and all communication with air traffic control was lost. The last known position of the plane was over the South China Sea, but subsequent analysis of satellite data suggested that the aircraft had deviated significantly from its planned route, flying westward across the Malay Peninsula and then southward over the Indian Ocean.

The search for Flight MH370 was unprecedented in its scale and complexity, involving multiple countries and utilizing cutting-edge technology. Despite these efforts, only a few pieces of debris, confirmed from the aircraft, have been found, washed up on the shores of the western Indian Ocean. The main wreckage and the black boxes, which could provide crucial information about the plane's final moments, have never been located.

Numerous theories have been proposed to explain the disappearance of Flight MH370, ranging from mechanical failure to hijacking and even pilot suicide. However, none of these theories have been conclusively proven, leaving the families of the passengers and crew members in a state of agonizing uncertainty.

The lack of concrete evidence has also given rise to many conspiracy theories, including the involvement of extraterrestrial forces, black holes, and secret military operations. While these theories may seem far-fetched, they are a testament to the enduring fascination and perplexity surrounding the case.

The disappearance of Flight MH370 serves as a stark reminder of the limits of human knowledge and technology, even in an age of unprecedented connectivity and information. As the years pass, the hope of finding definitive answers to this modern-day aviation enigma may be fading, but the quest for understanding continues. The mystery of Flight MH370 is a poignant reminder of the human desire to seek answers and make sense of the unexplained, even in the face of overwhelming odds.

The Bennington Triangle: A Series of Unexplained Disappearances in Vermont

Nestled in the picturesque Green Mountains of southwestern Vermont lies an area shrouded in mystery and intrigue. Dubbed the "Bennington Triangle" by paranormal author Joseph A. Citro, this region has been the site of a series of unexplained disappearances from the 1940s to the 1950s. The Bennington Triangle encompasses the towns of Bennington, Woodford, Shaftsbury, and Somerset, with Glastonbury Mountain at its center.

The first of these baffling vanishings occurred on November 12, 1945, when 74-year-old Middie Rivers, an experienced hunting guide, led a group of four hunters into the wilderness near Glastenbury Mountain. Rivers ventured ahead of the group on their return journey to scout the path, but he has yet to return. Despite an extensive search, no trace of Rivers was ever found, leaving many to wonder what could have happened to the seasoned woodsman.

The second disappearance occurred a year later, on December 1, 1946. Paula Welden, an 18-year-old college student, decided to take a hike on the Long Trail near Glastenbury Mountain. Witnesses reported seeing her on the trail but never returned to her dormitory that evening. A massive search effort involving over 1,000 people was launched, but no clues to her whereabouts were ever discovered. Welden's disappearance remains one of Vermont's most enduring mysteries.

The Bennington Triangle's eerie reputation grew in 1949 when James E. Tetford, a war veteran, vanished without a trace during a bus trip from St. Albans to Bennington. Tetford boarded the bus with 14 other passengers, but when the bus arrived in Bennington, he was nowhere to be found. His luggage and an open bus timetable were left behind on his seat, but there was no sign of Tetford himself.

The fourth and fifth disappearances occurred in 1950. On October 12, eight-year-old Paul Jepson vanished from his mother's truck while she tended to their pigs in Bennington. Despite a thorough search, including the use of bloodhounds, no trace of the boy was ever found. Just 16 days later, on October 28, Frieda Langer, a 53-year-old experienced hiker, disappeared during a hike near the Somerset Reservoir. Unlike the other cases, Langer's body was eventually found on May 12, 1951, in an area that had been searched extensively. However, due to the state of decomposition, no cause of death could be determined.

Theories surrounding these mysterious disappearances range from the plausible to the supernatural. Some speculate that the individuals fell victim to accidents or foul play, while others suggest that extraterrestrials abducted them or fell into hidden portals to other dimensions. Despite the passage of time, the enigma of the Bennington Triangle continues to captivate the imagination of locals and visitors alike, serving as a chilling reminder of the unknown forces that may lurk in the shadows of our world.

The Sodder Children: A Family's Unending Search for Answers

The Sodder family's story is one of heartache, determination, and an unyielding quest for the truth. In the early hours of Christmas Day in 1945, the Sodder family home in Fayetteville, West Virginia, was engulfed in flames. George and Jennie Sodder and four of their nine children managed to escape the inferno. However, five of their children, Maurice, Martha, Louis, Jennie, and Betty, aged between 5 and 14, seemingly vanished.

The fire department's response was slow, and by the time they arrived, the house had been reduced to ashes. Strangely, no remains of the missing children were found in the wreckage. The fire chief declared the fire an accident caused by faulty wiring, and the case was closed. However, the Sodder family refused to accept this explanation, believing their children had been abducted and the fire was a cover-up.

Over the years, the Sodders tirelessly pursued every lead and possible sighting of their missing children. They hired private investigators, offered rewards, and even erected a billboard near their former home detailing the case and pleading for information. Their efforts attracted national attention, and the case became one of the most enduring mysteries in American history.

Several factors fueled the Sodders' belief that their children were still alive. Firstly, the family received strange phone calls and visits in the weeks leading up to the fire, including a man who warned George that his house would be burned down and his children would be taken. Secondly, a witness claimed to have seen the children in a car driving away from the house on the night of the fire. Thirdly, a photograph of a young man resembling one of the missing children, Louis, was sent to the Sodders in 1968 with a cryptic message suggesting that he was still alive.

Despite these tantalizing clues, concrete evidence has yet to support the Sodders' theory. As a result, the case remains unsolved, and the fate of the five missing children is still unknown. The Sodder family's unending search for answers is a testament to the power of a parent's love and the human desire to uncover the truth behind life's most baffling mysteries.

The Yuba County Five: A Baffling Case of Vanished Friends

In February 1978, five friends from Yuba City, California, set out on a seemingly ordinary trip to attend a basketball game in Chico. Little did they know that this fateful journey would lead to one of American history's most perplexing and haunting mysteries. Known as the Yuba County Five, the baffling case of their disappearance continues to captivate and confound investigators and the public alike.

Gary Mathias, Jack Madruga, Jackie Huett, Theodore Weiher, and William Sterling were all young men in their 20s and 30s, each with varying degrees of intellectual disabilities or psychiatric issues. Yet, despite their challenges, they were a tight-knit group bonded by their shared love for sports and their participation in a local program for adults with special needs.

On the night of February 24, 1978, the friends piled into Madruga's Mercury Montego and drove 50 miles north to Chico to watch a college basketball game. After the game, they stopped at a convenience store to grab some snacks before beginning their journey home. Unfortunately, this seemingly innocuous pit stop would be the last time anyone saw the Yuba County Five alive.

When the men failed to return home the following day, their worried families reported them missing. A massive search and rescue operation was launched. Still, only a few days later was the first clue discovered: Madruga's abandoned car was found on a remote mountain road, far off their intended route and deep in the Plumas National Forest. The vehicle had gas in the tank and was in working order, but there was no sign of the men.

Over the next few months, search teams and volunteers scoured the rugged wilderness, but it wasn't until June that the first of the Yuba County Five was found. Weiher's emaciated body was discovered in a remote forest service trailer nearly 20 miles from the abandoned car. He had lost nearly half his body weight and had succumbed to hypothermia. Bizarrely, the trailer was stocked with ample food and heating supplies, but they had barely been touched.

In the following days, the remains of Madruga, Huett, and Sterling were found scattered throughout the surrounding area, each having met a similarly tragic fate. Unfortunately, the fifth group member, Gary Mathias, has never been found, and his ultimate fate remains a mystery.

The Yuba County Five case is riddled with perplexing questions: Why did the men abandon their car and venture into the wilderness on a freezing winter night? How did they become separated, and why didn't they use the available resources to survive? And what happened to Gary Mathias?

Despite the passage of time and numerous investigations, the enigma of the Yuba County Five remains unsolved. Their tragic story serves as a chilling reminder of the enduring fascination with vanishing acts and the impenetrable mysteries that continue to haunt us.

The Mysterious Disappearance of Malaysia's Jemaah Islamiyah Operatives

The enigma of unexplained disappearances is not limited to remote locations or historical events. In the modern era, the vanishing of individuals connected to clandestine organizations has continued to baffle investigators and spark public interest. One such case is the mysterious disappearance of Malaysia's Jemaah Islamiyah (JI) operatives, a group of individuals linked to a Southeast Asian militant Islamist organization.

Jemaah Islamiyah, which translates to "Islamic Congregation," was founded in the 1990s to establish an Islamic state across Southeast Asia. The organization has been linked to numerous terrorist attacks, including the 2002 Bali bombings that killed over 200 people. In the early 2000s, Malaysian authorities launched a crackdown on JI, arresting several key members and dismantling their operations.

However, some operatives managed to evade capture, and their whereabouts remain unknown.

One of the most prominent missing JI operatives is Mas Selamat Kastari, a Singaporean national who was believed to be the leader of JI's Singapore branch. Kastari was arrested in Indonesia in 2006 and extradited to Singapore, where he was detained under the Internal Security Act. In a shocking turn of events, Kastari escaped from a high-security detention center in 2008, sparking a massive search that spanned Southeast Asia. Despite extensive efforts by authorities, Kastari's whereabouts remain a mystery.

Another notable JI operative who vanished without a trace is Zulkifli Abdhir, also known as Marwan, a Malaysian national on the FBI's Most Wanted Terrorists list. Marwan was believed to be a key figure in JI's bomb-making operations and was linked to several terrorist attacks in the region. In 2015, Philippine authorities claimed that Marwan was killed in a raid, but his body was never recovered, and doubts about his death persist.

The disappearances of these JI operatives raise several questions: How have they managed to evade capture for so long? Are they still involved in terrorist activities or have they abandoned their extremist ideologies? Could they be receiving support from sympathizers or other militant groups? The lack of concrete answers to these questions only adds to the intrigue surrounding their vanishing acts.

As with other unexplained disappearances, the cases of the missing JI operatives remind us that even in our interconnected world, individuals can still vanish without a trace. The enduring fascination with these mysterious disappearances lies in the human desire to uncover the truth and make sense of the unknown. As long as questions remain unanswered, the enigma of the missing JI operatives and other unexplained vanishings will continue to captivate our collective imagination.

The Enduring Fascination with Vanishing Acts

As we reach the end of our journey through the world of unexplained disappearances, it is evident that these mysteries have captivated the human imagination for centuries. From the Lost Colony of Roanoke to the enigmatic case of Flight MH370, these stories continue to baffle and intrigue us. But what is it about these vanishing acts that hold such a powerful grip on our collective consciousness?

One reason for our enduring fascination with mysterious disappearances is the innate human desire to solve puzzles and uncover hidden truths. We are naturally drawn to the unknown, and our curiosity is piqued when faced with a perplexing enigma. We yearn to find answers and explanations to bring closure to these baffling cases. This drive to solve mysteries is deeply ingrained in our psyche, and this curiosity has led to countless advancements in science, technology, and our understanding of the world around us.

Another aspect of our fascination with unexplained disappearances lies in the emotional impact these stories have on us. The sudden and inexplicable loss of a loved one is a universal fear. When we hear of individuals or groups vanishing without a trace, we cannot help but empathize with the families and friends left behind. These stories serve as a stark reminder of the fragility of life and the uncertainty of our existence. They force us to confront our mortality and the possibility that we could one day vanish without explanation.

Moreover, mysterious disappearances often challenge our understanding of the world and the laws that govern it. When faced with cases that seemingly defy logic and reason, we question our assumptions and consider alternative explanations. This can lead to a sense of wonder and awe and a desire to explore the boundaries of our knowledge. In this way, unexplained disappearances can serve as a catalyst for intellectual growth and the expansion of our collective understanding.

Finally, the stories of mysterious disappearances often serve as cautionary tales, reminding us of the dangers that lurk in the world and the importance of staying vigilant. They teach us to be more aware of our surroundings, to take precautions when venturing into unfamiliar territory, and to never take our safety for granted. In this sense, these tales of vanishing acts can be seen as a form of collective learning, helping us to navigate the perils of our world and avoid the same tragic fate as those who have vanished before us.

In conclusion, the enduring fascination with unexplained disappearances is a testament to the complexity and depth of the human experience. These mysteries tap into our innate curiosity, empathy for others, desire for intellectual growth, and need for caution in an uncertain world. As long as there are unanswered questions and unsolved cases, our fascination with vanishing acts will persist, driving us to seek answers and, in doing so, to better understand ourselves and the world in which we live.

6

UNEXPLAINED PHENOMENA IN NATURE: EARTH'S PUZZLING WONDERS

Unexplained Phenomena in Nature

O ur planet is a treasure trove of wonders, brimming with awe-inspiring phenomena that captivate the human spirit and ignite our curiosity. From the highest peaks to the deepest depths, Earth's diverse landscapes and ecosystems are home to countless marvels that have fascinated scientists, explorers, and laypeople for centuries. Yet, amidst this vast array of natural spectacles, a select group of enigmas continues to elude explanation and defy our understanding. These unexplained mysteries, which we will delve into in this chapter, serve as humbling reminders of the limits of human knowledge and the infinite complexity of the natural world.

As we embark on this journey through Earth's puzzling wonders, we will encounter diverse phenomena that challenge conventional wisdom and confound scientific inquiry. From the twisted trunks of the Dancing Forest to the inexplicable movements of the Sailing Stones of Death Valley, these mysteries invite us to question our assumptions about the world and embrace the unknown with open minds and a sense of wonder.

In exploring these mysterious occurrences, we will also witness the extraordinary power of nature to create beauty and intrigue in the most unexpected places. The mesmerizing Hessdalen Lights, the eerie Taos Hum, and the perplexing patterns of Namibia's Fairy Circles are just a few examples of the astonishing phenomena that await us in the pages ahead.

As we dive deeper into these unexplained mysteries, we will also consider the broader implications of our quest for understanding. In a world where scientific advancements have illuminated so many aspects of our existence, these enduring enigmas serve as potent reminders of the vastness of the universe and the infinite potential for discovery that lies before us. They challenge us to push the boundaries of our knowledge, question the limits of our understanding, and embrace the thrill of the unknown.

So, let us embark on this journey together, with open minds and eager hearts, as we explore the enigma of nature's mysteries and celebrate the wonders of our incredible planet, for it is in the pursuit of these unexplained phenomena that we are reminded of the true beauty and complexity of the world around us and our enduring capacity for curiosity, wonder, and awe.

The Dancing Forest: Twisted Trees and Their Secrets

Nestled in the heart of the Curonian Spit, a UNESCO World Heritage Site that stretches between Russia and Lithuania lies a peculiar and enchanting forest that has captured the imagination of locals and visitors alike. Known as the Dancing Forest, this unique woodland is home to trees that twist, bend, and contort into various whimsical shapes and formations. The forest's enigmatic beauty has inspired countless tales and legends, but the actual cause of these arboreal acrobatics remains a mystery.

The Dancing Forest predominantly comprises Scots pines (Pinus sylvestris), a species known for its resilience and adaptability. However, the trees within this forest defy their brethren's typical straight and tall growth pattern. Instead, they spiral, loop, and weave themselves into a captivating dance, their trunks forming intricate patterns that defy nature's laws. Some trees even bend into complete circles, creating natural archways inviting visitors into this otherworldly realm.

Several theories have been proposed to explain the unusual growth patterns of the Dancing Forest's trees. One popular hypothesis suggests that the twisting may result from a genetic mutation within the local pine population. Others believe the trees' contortions could result from environmental factors, such as strong winds or unstable soil. Some even attribute the forest's peculiar appearance to the work of supernatural forces, with local legends claiming that the hands of ancient gods or mischievous spirits shaped the trees.

Another theory, rooted in science, points to the possibility of a unique symbiotic relationship between the trees and certain fungi. It is believed that these fungi may release chemicals that affect the trees' growth hormones, causing them to twist and bend in response. However, despite extensive research, concrete evidence has yet to conclusively support any of these theories.

Regardless of the cause, the Dancing Forest remains a testament to the power and mystery of nature. Its twisted trees remind us that our planet is full of unexplained phenomena that continue to captivate and intrigue us. As we wander through the forest's enchanting pathways, we are invited to embrace the unknown and appreciate the beauty of Earth's many wonders.

The Sailing Stones of Death Valley: A Geological Puzzle

In the heart of California's arid and unforgiving Death Valley lies a geological enigma that has captivated the minds of scientists and curious onlookers for decades. Known as the "Sailing Stones," these seemingly ordinary rocks have been found to move across the flat, dry surface of the Racetrack Playa, leaving behind long, winding trails etched into the cracked earth. The peculiar phenomenon has baffled experts and sparked numerous theories as the stones sail across the landscape without any apparent external force.

The Racetrack Playa, a dry lake bed nestled between towering mountain ranges, is an inhospitable environment characterized by scorching temperatures, minimal rainfall, and a desolate, barren land-scape. Here, the Sailing Stones have been observed to travel distances of up to several hundred meters, with some trails stretching as long as 1,500 feet. The stones vary in size and shape, ranging from small pebbles to large boulders weighing several hundred pounds.

For many years, the movement of the Sailing Stones remained a complete mystery, as no one had ever witnessed the stones in motion. Various theories were proposed, including the influence of magnetic fields, the action of wind and water, and even the involvement of extraterrestrial forces. However, none of these explanations fully account for the peculiar paths and patterns left behind by the stones.

It wasn't until 2014 that a team of researchers led by Richard Norris and James Norris finally cracked the code behind the Sailing Stones' mysterious journey. Using time-lapse photography and GPS tracking devices, the scientists could observe the stones in motion for the first time. Their findings revealed that a rare combination of natural factors was responsible for the stones' movement.

The researchers discovered that the Racetrack Playa occasionally experiences rainfall during the winter months, which fills the dry lake bed with a shallow layer of water. As nighttime temperatures plummet, the water freezes into thin sheets of ice, which encase the stones. When the sun rises, and the ice melts, the stones sit atop slippery, wet mud. At this point, even the gentlest of breezes can cause the ice-encased stones to slide across the surface, leaving behind their characteristic trails.

The Sailing Stones of Death Valley serve as a humbling reminder of the incredible power and complexity of the natural world. While science has managed to unravel the mystery behind their movement, these enigmatic stones inspire awe and wonder in all who witness their puzzling journey across the desolate landscape. As we explore the unexplained phenomena that abound on our planet, we are constantly reminded that there is still so much to learn and discover about the world in which we live.

The Mysterious Booming Sounds: The "Skyquakes" Phenomenon

Imagine a serene, quiet day when suddenly, the air is filled with a thunderous boom that seems to come from nowhere. This startling and unexplained phenomenon, known as "skyquakes," has been reported in various parts of the world for centuries. However, these mysterious booming sounds have left scientists, and researchers baffled as they continue to search for a plausible explanation.

Skyquakes, also called "mystery booms" or "atmospheric noises," are loud, explosive sounds seemingly emanating from the sky. These enigmatic noises have been reported globally, from the United States and Canada to Europe and Asia. The sounds have been described as similar to thunder, cannon fire, or sonic booms, yet no visible source or cause can be identified.

Several theories have been proposed to explain the origin of these puzzling sounds. One popular explanation is that skyquakes result from supersonic aircraft or military exercises, creating sonic booms as they break the sound barrier. However, this theory fails to account for the numerous instances where no aircraft or military activity has been reported near the skyquake.

Another possible explanation is that skyquakes are caused by meteorites entering the Earth's atmosphere, creating a sonic boom as they disintegrate. While this theory may explain some instances of skyquakes, it does not account for the regularity and frequency of the phenomenon in certain areas.

Some researchers have suggested that skyquakes may result from geological activity, such as earthquakes or volcanic eruptions. However, this theory is also met with skepticism, as many skyquakes have been reported in areas with little to no seismic or volcanic activity.

A more recent theory proposes that skyquakes may be caused by releasing natural gas from the Earth's crust. As the gas escapes into the atmosphere, it could create a loud, booming sound. This theory is supported by the fact that many skyquakes have been reported near bodies of water, where natural gas deposits are often found.

Despite the numerous theories, no definitive explanation for the skyquakes phenomenon has been found. As researchers continue to investigate this mysterious occurrence, the mystery booms remind us of the many unexplained wonders our planet has to offer. The skyquakes phenomenon is a testament to the fact that, even in our modern age of scientific discovery, there are still aspects of the natural world that remain shrouded in mystery, waiting to be unraveled and understood.

The Hessdalen Lights: Unexplained Luminous Aerial Displays

In the remote valley of Hessdalen, Norway, lies one of the most intriguing and inexplicable natural phenomena on Earth - the Hessdalen Lights. These mysterious luminous displays have captivated locals and scientists alike for decades with their ethereal beauty and mysterious origins. The lights, which appear as glowing orbs or elongated shapes, have been reported to hover, dance, and even dart across the night sky, leaving witnesses in awe and sparking numerous theories about their cause.

94

The Hessdalen Lights were first documented in the early 20th century, but it was in the 1980s that they gained widespread attention. During this period, the valley experienced a surge in sightings, with the lights appearing up to 20 times per week. This prompted a wave of curiosity and speculation, drawing researchers worldwide to study the phenomenon.

Despite extensive investigations, the exact cause of the Hessdalen Lights remains a mystery. Several theories have been proposed, ranging from natural explanations to more outlandish ideas. Some scientists believe the lights result from ionized gas particles, which become charged due to the valley's unique geology and create a luminous glow. Others suggest that the lights are a form of ball lightning, a rare and poorly understood atmospheric phenomenon.

More unconventional theories propose that the Hessdalen Lights result from extraterrestrial activity or a portal to another dimension. While these ideas may seem far-fetched, they highlight the enigmatic nature of the phenomenon and the human desire to seek answers to the unknown.

In recent years, the frequency of the Hessdalen Lights has decreased, with sightings occurring only a few times yearly. However, this has kept the fascination surrounding the phenomenon strong. Researchers continue to study the lights, hoping to unlock the secrets behind their elusive origins.

The Hessdalen Lights serve as a reminder of the many unexplained wonders that exist within our natural world. As we strive to understand these mysteries, we not only expand our knowledge of the world around us but also deepen our appreciation for the beauty and complexity of our planet. Ultimately, the most important lesson we can learn from the Hessdalen Lights is to embrace the unknown and never stop seeking answers to the questions that captivate our imagination.

The Taos Hum: A Perplexing Low-Frequency Sound

Nestled in the picturesque landscape of northern New Mexico, the small town of Taos has long been a haven for artists, writers, and spiritual seekers. However, since the early 1990s, it has also been the epicenter of an enigmatic auditory phenomenon known as the Taos Hum. This perplexing low-frequency sound has left scientists, researchers, and residents alike scratching their heads in search of an explanation.

The Taos Hum is described as a persistent, low-pitched hum akin to a diesel engine's distant rumble or an electrical transformer's buzzing. It is most often heard during the quiet hours of the night and is reported to be more intense indoors than outdoors. The hum has been a source of annoyance and distress for many residents, with some claiming that it has caused them physical discomfort and sleep disturbances.

Despite numerous investigations and studies, the origin of the Taos Hum remains a mystery. Some theories suggest that it could result from natural geological processes, such as the movement of tectonic plates or the release of underground gases. Others believe it may be caused by man-made sources, such as electrical power lines, communication towers, or even secret military experiments. However, no definitive evidence has been found to support any of these hypotheses.

One of the most intriguing aspects of the Taos Hum is that everyone in the area does not hear it. Only a small percentage of the population reports being able to perceive the sound. This has led some researchers to propose that the hum may be a form of tinnitus, a condition where individuals hear phantom noises without external sound sources. However, the fact that the hum is consistently described as having the same frequency and characteristics by those who hear it suggests that it is more than just a subjective auditory hallucination.

The Taos Hum is not an isolated phenomenon. Similar unexplained low-frequency sounds have been reported in other locations worldwide, including Bristol in the United Kingdom, Auckland in New Zealand, and Bondi in Australia. As a result, these mysterious hums have collectively come to be known as "Worldwide Hums," further fueling the intrigue and fascination surrounding these enigmatic auditory experiences.

As our understanding of the natural world and its complex interactions between its various elements continues to grow, we can one day unravel the mystery of the Taos Hum and its global counterparts. But, until then, the hum serves as a humbling reminder of the many wonders and enigmas that still await our discovery on this remarkable planet we call home.

The Devil's Kettle: A Waterfall That Swallows Rivers

Nestled within the lush wilderness of Minnesota's Judge C. R. Magney State Park lies a geological enigma that has baffled scientists and nature enthusiasts for decades. Known as the Devil's Kettle, this peculiar waterfall has captured the imagination of many, as it appears to swallow half of the Brule River without a trace. This section will delve into the enigmatic nature of the Devil's Kettle, exploring its unique characteristics and the theories surrounding its seemingly bottomless depths.

The Devil's Kettle waterfall is a fascinating spectacle, where the Brule River splits into two distinct channels. One channel cascades down a typical waterfall, eventually rejoining the river downstream. The other, however, takes a more mysterious route. It plunges into a large, rocky pothole, disappearing from sight and never resurfacing. Over the years, countless visitors have tossed in sticks, leaves, and even GPS trackers, hoping to uncover the water's final destination. Unfortunately, they have yet to be found downstream or anywhere else, leaving the fate of the swallowed water a perplexing mystery.

Several theories have been proposed to explain the Devil's Kettle's enigmatic behavior. One popular hypothesis suggests that the water is funneled into an underground river or aquifer, resurfacing elsewhere. However, this theory has been met with skepticism, as the region's geology is predominantly composed of volcanic rock, making the existence of a hidden underground river highly unlikely.

Another theory posits that porous rock may absorb the water beneath the waterfall, eventually rejoining the river through a series of underground channels. While this explanation seems plausible, it has yet to be proven. Researchers have conducted dye tests and other experiments to trace the water's path in recent years, but the results have been inconclusive, leaving the mystery of the Devil's Kettle unsolved.

Despite the lack of concrete answers, the Devil's Kettle continues to captivate the minds of those who encounter it. This enigmatic waterfall serves as a humbling reminder of our planet's many wonders and mysteries, waiting to be explored and appreciated. As we unravel the secrets of the natural world, we must also learn to embrace the unknown and appreciate the beauty and intrigue of phenomena like the Devil's Kettle. For it is in these unexplained mysteries that we find the inspiration to delve deeper into the complexities of our world, fostering a greater understanding and appreciation for the planet we call home.

The Fairy Circles of Namibia: Nature's Mysterious Patterns

In the arid grasslands of Namibia, a peculiar natural phenomenon has captivated the curiosity of scientists and laypeople alike for decades. Known as the Fairy Circles, these enigmatic patterns are characterized by circular patches of barren earth surrounded by a ring of thriving grass. Ranging from 2 to 15 meters in diameter, these otherworldly formations are scattered across the landscape, creating a mesmerizing sight that has inspired countless myths and legends.

The origin of the Fairy Circles has long been a debate among researchers, with various theories attempting to explain their existence. Some believe that the circles result from termites or ants, which clear the vegetation in their immediate vicinity to create a more favorable environment for their colonies. Others argue that the circles are the outcome of a natural process called self-organization, where plants compete for limited resources such as water and nutrients, forming distinct patterns in the vegetation.

One of the most intriguing aspects of the Fairy Circles is their remarkable uniformity and regularity. The circles are evenly spaced, with a consistent distance between neighboring formations. This has led some researchers to propose that the patterns result from an underground network of gas or water channels, which influence the distribution of nutrients in the soil and, consequently, vegetation growth.

Despite extensive research and numerous hypotheses, the actual cause of the Fairy Circles remains a mystery. Some scientists argue that a combination of factors, such as the interaction between termites and vegetation, may be responsible for the phenomenon. However, no single explanation has been universally accepted, and the enigma of the Fairy Circles continues to perplex and fascinate observers.

The Fairy Circles of Namibia serve as a powerful reminder of our planet's wonders and mysteries. These enigmatic formations challenge our understanding of the natural world and inspire us to delve deeper into the secrets of our environment. As we continue to explore and unravel the mysteries of the Fairy Circles, we are reminded that there is still much to learn about the complex and captivating world in which we live.

The Blood Falls of Antarctica: A Crimson Cascade in the Frozen World

In Antarctica's vast, icy expanse, a peculiar natural phenomenon has captured the attention of scientists and nature enthusiasts alike. Aptly named the Blood Falls, this striking cascade of crimson-hued liquid stands out in stark contrast against the pristine white snow and ice surrounding it. The sight of this mysterious waterfall, which seems to bleed from the very heart of the frozen continent, has intrigued and baffled observers for over a century.

The Blood Falls were first discovered in 1911 by Australian geologist and explorer Griffith Taylor, who stumbled upon the eerie sight during an expedition to the McMurdo Dry Valleys. The falls originate from the Taylor Glacier, a unique feature of the Antarctic landscape. Unlike most glaciers, the Taylor Glacier is a "cold-based" glacier, meaning it is frozen to the underlying bedrock and moves incredibly slowly. This peculiar characteristic plays a crucial role in forming the Blood Falls.

The source of the falls' distinctive red coloration for many years remained a mystery. Early theories suggested that the color was due to red algae, while others believed it to result from iron deposits in the surrounding rock. However, it wasn't until 2003 that researchers finally uncovered the actual cause of this enigmatic phenomenon.

The secret behind the Blood Falls lies in a subglacial lake trapped beneath the Taylor Glacier. This ancient body of water, which has been sealed off from the outside world for millions of years, contains an unusually high concentration of iron. As the glacier slowly grinds against the bedrock, it scrapes away at the iron-rich rock, releasing a mixture of water and iron particles. When this iron-rich water finally escapes the glacier and comes into contact with the oxygen in the air, it undergoes a chemical reaction that causes the iron particles to rust, turning the water a deep, blood-red color.

But the story of the Blood Falls continues. In addition to its striking appearance, this natural wonder also harbors a unique and thriving ecosystem. The subglacial lake that feeds the falls is home to a community of extremophile microorganisms, which have adapted to survive in the dark, oxygen-deprived, and nutrient-poor environment. These hardy microbes derive their energy from the chemical reactions between the iron and sulfur in the water, a process known as chemosynthesis. The discovery of life in such an inhospitable environment has not only expanded our understanding of the limits of life on Earth. Still, it has also raised intriguing questions about the possibility of life on other planets.

The Blood Falls of Antarctica is a vivid reminder of the countless mysteries that still await discovery on our planet. With its unique geological origins and hidden ecosystem, this enigmatic crimson cascade continues to captivate and inspire those fortunate enough to witness its eerie beauty. As we continue to explore and unravel the secrets of Earth's natural wonders, we are reminded of the limitless potential for surprise and wonder hidden within the world around us.

The Great Blue Hole: A Submerged Sinkhole with Hidden Depths

The Great Blue Hole is a captivating natural wonder that has captured the imagination of scientists, explorers, and tourists alike. Located off the coast of Belize, this massive underwater sinkhole is a geological marvel that has remained mysterious for centuries. The Great Blue Hole is a stunning visual spectacle and a treasure trove of scientific intrigue as researchers continue to delve into its depths to uncover its secrets.

The Great Blue Hole is a circular, deep blue abyss that spans approximately 1,000 feet in diameter and plunges to over 400 feet. This enigmatic formation is part of the more extensive Belize Barrier Reef Reserve System, a UNESCO World Heritage Site. The hole's striking appearance is due to the contrast between the shallow, crystal-clear waters surrounding it and the sinkhole's dark, seemingly bottomless depths.

The origins of the Great Blue Hole date back to the last ice age, approximately 15,000 years ago. It is believed that the sinkhole was initially formed as a limestone cave system, which eventually collapsed due to rising sea levels. Over time, the ocean's waters filled the void, creating the mesmerizing underwater chasm we see today.

Despite its alluring beauty, the Great Blue Hole remains a largely unexplored frontier. The sinkhole's depth and challenging diving conditions have made it difficult for researchers to thoroughly study its underwater ecosystem and geological features. However, recent technological advances have allowed scientists to venture deeper into the hole, revealing a complex network of submerged caves, stalactites, and other geological formations.

The Great Blue Hole is also home to diverse marine life, including various species of sharks, rays, and fish. The unique environment within the sinkhole has given rise to a distinct ecosystem, with many species adapted to the low-light, low-oxygen conditions found at its depths. This has led scientists to believe that the Great Blue Hole may hold the key to understanding the evolution of marine life and the Earth's changing climate over time.

The allure of the Great Blue Hole extends beyond its scientific significance. The sinkhole has become a popular destination for divers and adventure seekers, drawn to its mysterious depths and the opportunity to explore a truly unique underwater landscape. The Great Blue

Hole serves as a reminder of the Earth's immense power to create awe-inspiring natural wonders and the enduring mysteries that lie beneath the surface of our planet.

In conclusion, the Great Blue Hole is a testament to the Earth's capacity for creating breathtaking and mysterious phenomena. As we continue to explore and study this underwater marvel, we are reminded of the importance of preserving and appreciating the wonders of our natural world. The Great Blue Hole stands as a symbol of the unexplained mysteries that still await discovery, inspiring curiosity and a sense of wonder in all who gaze upon its mysterious depths.

The Naga Fireballs: Mysterious Glowing Orbs Rising from the Mekong River

The Mekong River, one of Asia's longest and most significant rivers, holds a fascinating secret that has captivated locals and visitors alike for centuries. Every year, during the full moon in October, a strange and mesmerizing phenomenon occurs along a stretch of the river between Thailand and Laos. As the sun sets and darkness envelops the riverbanks, thousands of glowing orbs mysteriously rise from the depths of the Mekong River and ascend into the night sky. These mysterious fireballs, known as the Naga Fireballs or "bung fai paya nak" in Thai, have been the subject of wonder, awe, and scientific curiosity for generations.

The Naga Fireballs are named after the mythical serpent-like creatures called "Nagas" that are believed to inhabit the Mekong River. According to local folklore, these supernatural beings shoot fireballs into the sky to celebrate the end of Buddhist Lent, a period of spiritual reflection and self-discipline. The fireballs are said to be a manifestation of the Nagas' immense power and a reminder of the mystical forces that dwell beneath the surface of our world.

While the Naga Fireballs have long been a part of local legend and tradition, the phenomenon has also attracted scientists and researchers seeking to unravel the mystery behind these glowing orbs. Several theories have been proposed to explain the fireballs, ranging from the release of flammable gases produced by decomposing organic matter on the riverbed to the presence of phosphine gas, which can ignite spontaneously when exposed to air. However, none of these theories have been conclusively proven, and the Naga Fireballs continue to baffle and intrigue experts.

Despite the lack of a definitive scientific explanation, the Naga Fireballs have become an important cultural and spiritual event for the people living along the Mekong River. Every year, thousands of locals and tourists gather on the riverbanks to witness the spectacle, with many participating in the Naga Fireball Festival. This celebration includes traditional music, dance, and prayers. For the people of the Mekong, the fireballs are not just a fascinating natural enigma but also a symbol of the enduring connection between their communities, their beliefs, and the mysterious forces of nature.

As we continue to explore and seek to understand the many unexplained phenomena that occur on our planet, the Naga Fireballs stand as a testament to the enduring allure of the unknown. These mysterious orbs of light, rising from the depths of the Mekong River, remind us that countless mysteries are still waiting to be discovered and that the world we inhabit is far more complex and wondrous than we could ever imagine.

Embracing the Wonders and Mysteries of Our Planet

As we reach the end of our journey through nature's unexplained mysteries, it is essential to take a moment to reflect on the significance of these enigmatic phenomena. From the twisted trees of the Dancing Forest to the mesmerizing depths of the Great Blue Hole, these natural wonders remind us that our planet is an ever-evolving, dynamic, and mysterious place.

The Earth is a treasure trove of secrets waiting to be discovered, and the unexplained phenomena we have explored in this chapter are just a tiny sample of the countless mysteries that lie hidden within its depths. These wonders remind us that, despite our advances in technology and scientific understanding, there is still so much we do not know about the world around us.

Embracing our planet's mysteries is an invitation to explore and learn and an opportunity to cultivate a sense of wonder and curiosity. By acknowledging that there are still unsolved puzzles in nature, we open ourselves to discoveries and insights that can enrich our lives and deepen our connection to the Earth.

Moreover, these unexplained phenomena remind us of the importance of preserving and protecting our planet's natural wonders. As we continue to unravel the mysteries of the Earth, we must also recognize our responsibility to safeguard its delicate ecosystems and diverse habitats. Doing so ensures that future generations can experience the awe and wonder these mysterious phenomena inspire.

In conclusion, the unexplained mysteries of nature serve as a humbling reminder of the vastness and complexity of our planet. They invite us to look beyond the familiar and delve into the unknown, to question our assumptions and embrace the enigma of the natural world. By doing so, we enrich our understanding of the Earth and foster a deeper appreciation for the beauty and wonder within its many mysteries. As we continue to explore and uncover the secrets of our planet, let us remember to cherish and protect the wonders that make our world such a remarkable and mysterious place.

7

TIME SLIPS AND PARALLEL UNIVERSES: THE FABRIC OF REALITY

Time Slips and Parallel Universes

I magine, for a moment, that you are walking down a familiar street when suddenly, everything around you changes. The people, the buildings, and even the air feel different. You have just experienced a time slip, a phenomenon that has captivated the minds of scientists, paranormal investigators, and ordinary people for centuries. Time slips are often described as sudden and temporary shifts in time and space, transporting an individual to a different era or reality. But are time slips merely the stuff of science fiction, or do they provide a glimpse into the true nature of our universe?

On the other hand, parallel universes are a concept that physicists and philosophers have long debated. The idea that there may be multiple coexisting realities, each with unique circumstances and outcomes, is fascinating and mind-boggling. Could our decisions and actions in this reality have a ripple effect on countless other realities? And if so, what does this mean for our understanding of the world and our place within it?

This chapter will delve into ten mysteries of time slips and parallel universes. As we embark on this journey through time and space, we will also consider the role of human perception in shaping our experiences of these phenomena. For example, are time slips and encounters with parallel universes simply the result of our minds playing tricks on us, or do they offer a window into a deeper, more complex understanding of the fabric of reality? And as we continue to push the boundaries of scientific knowledge, what discoveries await us in our quest to unravel the enigma of time slips and parallel universes?

Join us as we venture into the unknown, exploring the captivating world of time slips and parallel universes and uncovering the secrets that lie at the very heart of our existence.

The Moberly-Jourdain Incident

The Moberly-Jourdain Incident, also known as the Ghosts of Petit Trianon or the Versailles Time Slip, is a fascinating and mysterious event on August 10, 1901. Two British women, Charlotte Anne Moberly, and Eleanor Jourdain, claimed to have experienced a time slip while visiting the Palace of Versailles in France. Their account of the incident has intrigued historians, paranormal researchers, and enthusiasts of the unexplained for over a century.

Charlotte Anne Moberly was the principal of St. Hugh's College, Oxford, while Eleanor Jourdain was a writer and educator. The two women were visiting Paris and decided to spend a day exploring the Palace of Versailles and its gardens. They were particularly interested in visiting the Petit Trianon, a small chateau on the palace grounds that was once the private retreat of Marie Antoinette.

As they wandered the gardens, Moberly and Jourdain became disoriented and found themselves on an unfamiliar path. They soon noticed that their surroundings seemed to have changed, with the landscape appearing more wild and unkempt than the meticulously maintained gardens they had been walking through. In addition, the atmosphere felt oppressive, and they encountered several people dressed in clothing that appeared to be from the late 18th century.

The women continued on their way, eventually reaching the Petit Trianon. However, they later discovered that the people they had encountered were not part of any historical reenactment or event. Instead, Moberly and Jourdain became convinced that they had somehow slipped back in time and experienced the gardens as they were during the reign of Marie Antoinette.

In 1911, the two women published a book about their experience, titled "An Adventure." The book detailed their encounter with the strange surroundings and people, including a man they believed to be the Comte de Vaudreuil, a close friend of Marie Antoinette, and a woman who resembled the queen herself.

The Moberly-Jourdain Incident has been the subject of much debate and speculation since the publication of their book. Some researchers believe that the women experienced a time slip, a phenomenon in which individuals seemingly travel through time without apparent cause. Others suggest that the incident resulted from the women's vivid imaginations or a shared hallucination.

Skeptics have pointed out inconsistencies in Moberly and Jourdain's accounts and questioned the reliability of their memories. Some have proposed that the women may have stumbled upon a historical reenactment or a costume party, which they later misremembered as a genuine time slip experience.

Despite the many theories and explanations, the Moberly-Jourdain Incident remains an enigmatic and captivating tale. It continues to capture the imagination of those interested in the unexplained and is a fascinating example of the enduring allure of time travel and parallel universes.

The Philadelphia Experiment

The Philadelphia Experiment is a controversial and widely debated event that allegedly took place during World War II. According to the legend, the United States Navy conducted a top-secret experiment in 1943 involving the USS Eldridge, a destroyer escort ship. The objective of the experiment was to render the ship invisible to enemy radar, using advanced technology based on electromagnetic fields and unified field theory. However, the story goes that the experiment had unintended consequences, resulting in the ship's teleportation, time displacement, and other bizarre phenomena.

The origins of the Philadelphia Experiment can be traced back to a series of letters sent to UFO researcher Morris K. Jessup in the 1950s. The letters were written by a man named Carlos Allende, who claimed to have witnessed the experiment while serving on a nearby ship, the SS Andrew Furuseth. Allende described how the USS Eldridge vanished from its location in the Philadelphia Naval Shipyard and reappeared moments later in Norfolk, Virginia, before returning to Philadelphia.

According to Allende, the experiment had disastrous effects on the crew aboard the USS Eldridge. Some were said to have been fused to the ship's hull, while others suffered severe mental trauma, disorientation, and even invisibility. Allende's letters also mentioned the involvement of renowned physicist Albert Einstein, who was allegedly working on the unified field theory at the time.

The story of the Philadelphia Experiment gained widespread attention in the 1960s and 1970s, fueled by conspiracy theories, books, and eventually a 1984 movie adaptation. As a result, the alleged event has been the subject of much debate and investigation, with many researchers attempting to uncover the truth behind the claims.

Skeptics argue that the Philadelphia Experiment is nothing more than a hoax or an urban legend, pointing to Allende's account's lack of concrete evidence and inconsistencies. The U.S. Navy has consistently denied involvement in such an experiment, stating that the USS Eldridge was never equipped with the technology described by Allende and that the ship's logs show no indication of any unusual events during the time in question.

Some researchers have suggested that the story may have been inspired by experiments conducted during World War II, such as the development of degaussing technology to protect ships from magnetic mines. However, these experiments were far less dramatic and did not involve teleportation or time travel.

Despite the lack of definitive evidence, the Philadelphia Experiment continues to captivate the imagination of conspiracy theorists, paranormal enthusiasts, and those interested in the unexplained. The story is a compelling example of the enduring fascination with secret government projects, advanced technology, and the potential consequences of tampering with the unknown.

The Vanishing Hotel

The Vanishing Hotel is a mysterious and intriguing story in 1979 involving two British couples who claimed to have experienced a time slip while traveling in France. The incident has captured the imagination of paranormal enthusiasts and those interested in unexplained phenomena. It raises questions about the nature of time, reality, and the existence of parallel universes.

Geoff and Pauline Simpson and their friends Len and Cynthia Gisby were on a road trip through France when they decided to find a hotel for the night. After consulting a guidebook, they chose a hotel in the small town of Montelimar. However, as they approached the town, they found themselves on an unfamiliar road leading them away from their intended destination.

As they continued driving, they came across a quaint, old-fashioned hotel not listed in their guidebook. Deciding to stay there for the night, the couples were struck by the hotel's antiquated appearance and the staff's outdated clothing. The rooms had no modern amenities, such as telephones or television sets, and the windows were fitted with wooden shutters instead of glass.

The next morning, the couples paid their bill, which was surprisingly low, and continued on their journey. They took several photographs of the hotel, intending to show their friends and family back home. However, they were still looking for it when they tried to return to the hotel on their way back through France. The road they had previously taken seemed to have vanished, and there was no sign of the hotel or any landmarks they had seen during their stay.

Upon returning to England, the couples were shocked to discover that their photographs of the hotel were missing from their camera. They contacted the French authorities and the guidebook publishers to inquire about the hotel, but they were still waiting for a record of its existence.

The story of the Vanishing Hotel has been the subject of much speculation and debate. Some believe the couples experienced a time slip, a phenomenon in which individuals seemingly travel through time without apparent cause. In this case, the couples may have been transported back to the early 20th century, when they encountered the hotel as it existed in the past.

Others have suggested that the incident resulted from the couples' vivid imaginations or a shared hallucination, possibly influenced by fatigue or the stress of traveling in a foreign country. Skeptics have also pointed out the need for concrete evidence, such as the missing photographs, and questioned the reliability of the couples' memories.

Despite the many theories and explanations, the Vanishing Hotel remains an enigmatic and captivating tale. It is a fascinating example of the enduring allure of unexplained phenomena and the mysteries of time and reality.

The Montauk Project

The Montauk Project is a series of alleged secret government experiments at Camp Hero, a former military base in Montauk, New York. The project was conducted during the 1970s and 1980s, primarily developing advanced psychological warfare techniques and researching the potential for time travel, teleportation, and contact with parallel universes. The Montauk Project has become popular among conspiracy theorists, paranormal enthusiasts, and those interested in the unexplained. It raises questions about the extent of government secrecy and the potential consequences of tampering with the unknown.

The origins of the Montauk Project can be traced back to the 1984 publication of "The Montauk Project: Experiments in Time" by Preston B. Nichols and Peter Moon. The book claims that the project was a continuation of the Philadelphia Experiment, a rumored US Navy experiment in 1943 that allegedly resulted in the teleportation and time displacement of the USS Eldridge. According to Nichols and Moon, the Montauk Project was an attempt to explore further the technology and phenomena discovered during the Philadelphia Experiment.

The experiments conducted at Camp Hero are said to have involved a wide range of subjects, including mind control, telepathy, and manipulating electromagnetic fields. One of the most famous claims associated with the Montauk Project is the creation of a "time tunnel," which allowed researchers to travel through time and space. The project is also said to have involved contact with extraterrestrial beings and exploring alternate dimensions.

Several individuals claim to have been involved in the Montauk Project, including Al Bielek, who stated that he participated in both the Philadelphia Experiment and the Montauk Project. Bielek claimed that he and his brother, Duncan Cameron, were sent through the time tunnel to various points in history, including 2137 and the 28th century.

Skeptics argue that the Montauk Project is nothing more than a hoax or an urban legend, pointing to the lack of concrete evidence and the implausibility of many of the claims made by those involved. The US government has consistently denied involvement in such experiments, and no official records of the Montauk Project have ever been found.

Despite lacking definitive evidence, the Montauk Project continues to captivate the imagination of conspiracy theorists and paranormal enthusiasts. The story has inspired numerous books, documentaries, and even a popular Netflix series, "Stranger Things," which draws heavily from the alleged events at Camp Hero. The Montauk Project is a compelling example of the enduring fascination with secret government projects, advanced technology, and the potential dangers of exploring the unknown.

The Berenstain Bears Effect

The Berenstain Bears Effect, also known as the Mandela Effect, is a phenomenon where a large number of people remember an event, fact, or detail differently than it actually occurred or exists. In the case of the Berenstain Bears, many people recall the popular children's book series and its associated television shows and merchandise as being spelled "Berenstein Bears," with an "e," rather than the correct spelling, "Berenstain Bears," with an "a." This widespread discrepancy in memory has led to various theories and speculations about the nature of reality, memory, and the possibility of parallel universes.

The Berenstain Bears, created by Stan and Jan Berenstain, first appeared in 1962 and became a beloved staple of children's literature. The confusion over the spelling of the name has puzzled and intrigued both casual observers and researchers alike. Some attribute the discrepancy to simple misremembering or the commonality of "-stein" as a suffix in surnames, causing people to assume the incorrect spelling.

However, more elaborate theories have emerged to explain the Berenstain Bears Effect. One such theory suggests that the discrepancy in memory is evidence of the existence of parallel universes or alternate realities. According to this theory, those who remember the name "Berenstein Bears" may have experienced a shift between two parallel universes, one in which the name is spelled with an "e" and another in which it is spelled with an "a." This idea is often linked to the broader concept of the Mandela Effect, named after the false memory some people have of Nelson Mandela dying in prison during the 1980s, despite his actual death occurring in 2013.

Another theory posits that the Berenstain Bears Effect results from collective false memory, a phenomenon where a group of people remembers an event or detail inaccurately, often due to the influence of external factors or the reinforcement of the false memory by others. This theory suggests that the widespread misremembering of the name may have been perpetuated through social interactions, media, and other sources, reinforcing the incorrect spelling in people's minds.

While the Berenstain Bears Effect remains an intriguing and unexplained phenomenon, it is a fascinating example of the complexities of human memory and the power of collective belief. Whether the result of parallel universes, collective false memory, or simple misremembering, the Berenstain Bears Effect continues to captivate the imagination and spark debate among those interested in the mysteries of the mind and the nature of reality.

The John Titor Story

The John Titor Story is a fascinating and enigmatic tale that emerged in the early 2000s, involving a person claiming to be a time traveler from 2036. The story captured the attention of internet users, conspiracy theorists, and those interested in the unexplained. It raised questions about the nature of time travel, the future of humanity, and the possibility of alternate realities.

The story began in November 2000 when a user named "TimeTravel_0" appeared on an online forum discussing time travel and other paranormal topics. The user claimed to be a time traveler from 2036, sent back to 1975 to retrieve an IBM 5100 computer, which was needed to debug aging computer systems in the future. The time traveler later identified himself as John Titor and began sharing detailed information about future events, technology, and his experiences as a time traveler.

John Titor provided a wealth of information about the future, including predictions about upcoming political, social, and environmental events. Some of his most notable predictions included a second American Civil War beginning in 2004, followed by a global nuclear conflict in 2015. Titor also described advanced technology in his time, such as the time machine he claimed to have traveled in, which was supposedly built by General Electric and utilized miniature black holes to bend time and space.

As Titor continued to share his story and answer questions from forum users, he gained a significant following, with many people captivated by his detailed accounts and apparent knowledge of future events. However, as time passed and Titor's predictions failed to come true, skepticism about his claims grew.

Some researchers and enthusiasts have attempted to uncover the truth behind the John Titor story, with various theories emerging about his identity and the veracity of his claims. Some believe that Titor was a hoax perpetrated by a clever individual or group seeking to create an elaborate and engaging internet legend. Others suggest that Titor may have been a genuine time traveler but that his presence in our timeline altered the course of events, causing his predictions to become inaccurate.

Despite the many theories and explanations, the John Titor story remains enigmatic and captivating. It is a fascinating example of the enduring allure of time travel, the power of the internet to create and perpetuate legends, and the human fascination with the unknown and the future.

The Man from Taured

The Man from Taured is a mysterious and intriguing story that allegedly occurred in 1954 at Tokyo's Haneda Airport. The incident involves a man who claimed to be from a country called Taured, which did not exist on any map or in any historical records. The story has captivated the imagination of conspiracy theorists, paranormal enthusiasts, and those interested in unexplained phenomena. It raises questions about the nature of reality, parallel universes' existence, and human memory's reliability.

According to the story, the man arrived at Haneda Airport on a flight from Europe and presented a passport from the non-existent country of Taured when going through customs. The passport appeared genuine, with visa stamps from previous visits to Japan and other countries. However, when questioned by airport officials, the man became increasingly agitated and insisted that Taured was a real country between France and Spain.

The man was taken into custody for further questioning, and a map was presented to him in an attempt to identify his country of origin. He pointed to where the Principality of Andorra is located but insisted that it was Taured, a country he claimed had existed for over a thousand years. The man spoke several languages, including Japanese, and appeared to be a well-traveled businessman.

Airport officials, unable to verify the man's identity or the existence of Taured, decided to detain him in a nearby hotel under the supervision of immigration officers while they investigated his claims. However, the next morning, the man vanished without a trace, despite the room being under constant surveillance. His passport and personal belongings had also disappeared, leaving no evidence of his existence.

The story of the Man from Taured has been the subject of much speculation and debate. Some believe the man was a genuine visitor from a parallel universe where Taured exists as a real country. According to this theory, the man may have accidentally crossed over into our reality, only to be pulled back into his universe when he disappeared.

Others suggest that the incident was a hoax or an urban legend, possibly inspired by real cases of individuals with false or altered passports attempting to enter a country. Finally, skeptics have pointed out the need for concrete evidence, such as official records or documentation of the incident, and questioned the story's reliability as it has been passed down through various retellings.

Despite the many theories and explanations, the Man from Taured remains an enigmatic and captivating tale. It is a fascinating example of the enduring allure of unexplained phenomena and the mysteries of alternate realities and parallel universes.

The Mandela Effect

The Mandela Effect is a phenomenon in which a large number of people remember an event, fact, or detail differently than it actually occurred or exists. The term was coined by paranormal researcher Fiona Broome in 2010, who discovered that she and many others shared a false memory of the South African leader Nelson Mandela dying in prison during the 1980s. In reality, Mandela was released from prison in 1990 and became the President of South Africa before passing away in 2013. This discrepancy in collective memory has led to various theories and speculations about the nature of reality, memory, and the possibility of parallel universes.

The Mandela Effect extends beyond the specific case of Nelson Mandela's death, with numerous other examples of collective false memories being reported. Some well-known instances include the misremembering of the spelling of the children's book series "The Berenstain Bears" as "The Berenstein Bears," the location of New Zealand in relation to Australia, and the famous line from the movie "Snow White and the Seven Dwarfs," which is often misquoted as "Mirror, mirror on the wall" instead of the correct "Magic mirror on the wall."

Several theories have been proposed to explain the Mandela Effect. One such theory suggests that the phenomenon is evidence of parallel universes or alternate realities. According to this theory, those who remember events or details differently may have experienced a shift between two parallel universes, causing their memories to become misaligned with their current reality.

Another theory posits that the Mandela Effect results from a collective false memory. In this phenomenon, a group of people remembers an event or detail inaccurately, often due to the influence of external factors or the reinforcement of false memory by others. This theory suggests that widespread misremembering may be perpetuated through social interactions, media, and other sources, reinforcing the false memory in people's minds.

Cognitive psychologists also offer explanations based on the fallibility of human memory and the brain's tendency to fill in gaps or create narratives that make sense of incomplete or ambiguous information. In addition, factors such as confirmation bias, suggestibility, and the power of suggestion can all contribute to the formation and reinforcement of false memories.

While the Mandela Effect remains an intriguing and unexplained phenomenon, it is a fascinating example of the complexities of human memory and the power of collective belief. Whether the result of parallel universes, collective false memory, or the fallibility of human memory, the Mandela Effect continues to captivate the imagination and spark debate among those interested in the mysteries of the mind and the nature of reality.

The Time-Traveling Hipster

The Time-Traveling Hipster is a curious and captivating story that emerged on the internet in 2010, involving a photograph from 1941 that appears to show a man dressed in modern clothing. The photograph, taken at the reopening of the South Fork Bridge in Gold Bridge, British Columbia, has sparked numerous debates and theories about the nature of time travel, the existence of parallel universes, and the possibility of anachronisms in historical records.

In the photograph, a man stands among a crowd dressed in typical 1940s attire. However, the man appears to be wearing modern sunglasses, a printed t-shirt, and a hoodie, all of which seem out of place for the time period. This striking contrast has led many to speculate that the man is a time traveler who somehow found himself in the past or evidence of a parallel universe where fashion trends developed differently.

Several theories have been proposed to explain the Time-Traveling Hipster phenomenon. Some believe the man is a real-time traveler, accidentally captured in a photograph while visiting the past. Others suggest that the photograph is evidence of a parallel universe, where the man's clothing is representative of the fashion trends of that alternate reality.

Skeptics, however, argue that the Time-Traveling Hipster is simply a misinterpretation or an optical illusion. They point out that the sunglasses worn by the man were available in the 1940s, albeit less common, and that his clothing could be explained by the fact that some casual or sportswear items, such as hoodies and printed t-shirts, were also in existence at the time, though not as widespread as they are today. Additionally, some have suggested that the photograph may have been digitally manipulated or altered in some way to create the appearance of an anachronism.

Despite the various theories and explanations, the Time-Traveling Hipster remains an enigmatic and intriguing story. It is a fascinating example of the enduring allure of unexplained phenomena, the mysteries of time travel, and the power of the internet to create and perpetuate legends. Whether the result of a real-time traveler, a parallel universe, or simply a misinterpretation of historical fashion, the Time-Traveling Hipster continues to captivate the imagination and spark debate among those interested in the mysteries of time and reality.

The Double Slit Experiment

The Double Slit Experiment is a groundbreaking quantum physics experiment that demonstrates particles' strange behavior at the quantum level, challenging our understanding of the nature of reality and the fundamental principles of classical physics. First performed by Thomas Young in 1801 and later refined by various physicists, the experiment played a crucial role in developing quantum mechanics. It has provided evidence of wave-particle duality and the observer effect.

The experiment involves shining a beam of light (or other particles, such as electrons) through two parallel slits in a barrier and observing the pattern that forms on a screen behind the barrier. According to classical physics, one would expect to see two distinct bands of light on the screen, corresponding to the light passing through each slit. However, the actual result of the experiment is an interference pattern similar to what would be observed if two waves were interacting. This suggests that the particles behave simultaneously as particles and waves, a phenomenon known as wave-particle duality.

The truly puzzling aspect of the Double Slit Experiment arises when the particles are sent through the slits one at a time. However, even when individual particles are sent through the slits, the interference pattern still appears on the screen, as if each particle somehow interferes with itself. This suggests that the particles exist in multiple states simultaneously, a concept known as superposition in quantum mechanics.

The experiment becomes even more intriguing when an observer attempts to measure which slit the particle passes through. When a measurement is made, the interference pattern disappears, and the particles behave as if they are only passing through one slit, as classical physics would predict. This phenomenon, known as the observer effect or the collapse of the wave function, implies that the act of observation or measurement directly impacts particles' behavior at the quantum level.

The Double Slit Experiment has profound implications for our understanding of the nature of reality and the role of the observer in shaping that reality. It has led to the development of various interpretations of quantum mechanics, such as the Copenhagen interpretation, which posits that particles exist in a state of superposition until they are measured, and the Many Worlds interpretation, which suggests that every possible outcome of a quantum event exists in a separate, parallel universe.

In conclusion, the Double Slit Experiment is a cornerstone of quantum physics that has challenged our understanding of the fundamental principles of the universe and opened the door to a world of seemingly impossible phenomena, such as superposition, wave-particle duality, and the observer effect. Moreover, the experiment continues to captivate the imagination of scientists and laypeople as a powerful reminder of the mysteries that remain uncovered in quantum mechanics.

The Enduring Mystery of Time Slips and Parallel Universes

As we reach the end of our exploration into the mysterious world of time slips and parallel universes, we must acknowledge that these phenomena remain shrouded in mystery. Despite the numerous accounts, scientific theories, and popular culture references, we still need to understand these occurrences' true nature fully. However, this lack of concrete answers only fuels our curiosity and fascination.

In sharing personal accounts and experiences, we have provided a glimpse into the lives of those who have encountered time slips and parallel universes firsthand. These stories remind us that, while we may not yet have all the answers, searching for understanding is a journey worth undertaking.

As we continue to unravel the mysteries of time slips and parallel universes, it is essential to approach the subject with an open mind, a sense of wonder, and a willingness to embrace the unknown, for it is in the pursuit of knowledge and the exploration of the unexplained that we genuinely push the boundaries of human understanding and expand our perception of reality.

In conclusion, time slips and parallel universes remain an enduring mystery that captivates the imagination of scientists, researchers, and the general public. As we continue to probe the depths of our universe and the fabric of reality, we can only hope that one day, we will unlock the secrets of these phenomena and gain a deeper understanding of the world in which we live. So let us revel in the mystery and marvel at the infinite possibilities beyond our grasp.

8

MYSTERIOUS ARTIFACTS: OUT-OF-PLACE AND OUT-OF-TIME DISCOVERIES

Mysterious Artifacts

Throughout human history, countless artifacts have been discovered that defy conventional explanations. These mysterious objects, often called out-of-place artifacts (OOParts), challenge our understanding of the past and force us to reconsider the timeline of human development. Some of these artifacts are far more advanced than the technology of their time, while others depict events or creatures that should not have existed in the era they were created. The enigma of these unexplained artifacts has captivated the imagination of historians, archaeologists, and enthusiasts alike, leading to many theories and speculations.

The allure of these artifacts lies in their ability to challenge our preconceived notions about the past. They serve as tantalizing clues to a hidden history that may be far more complex and fascinating than we ever imagined. As we explore into the mysteries surrounding these objects, we are forced to confront the limitations of our knowledge and consider the possibility that there may be more to our world than meets the eye.

This chapter will explore some of the most intriguing and enigmatic artifacts ever discovered. From ancient astronomical computers to cryptic texts that have yet to be deciphered, these objects have baffled experts for decades, if not centuries. We will examine the theories and controversies surrounding these artifacts and the implications they hold for our understanding of human history.

As we embark on this journey through the realm of unexplained artifacts, it is important to approach these mysteries with an open mind and a healthy dose of skepticism. While it is tempting to attribute these objects to lost civilizations or extraterrestrial visitors, it is crucial to consider all possible explanations and weigh the evidence carefully. In doing so, we may come one step closer to unraveling the enigma of these out-of-place and out-of-time discoveries, shedding light on the hidden corners of our past and expanding our understanding of the world in which we live.

The Antikythera Mechanism: An Ancient Astronomical Computer

The Antikythera Mechanism is one of the most fascinating and enigmatic artifacts ever discovered. This ancient Greek device, found in a shipwreck off the coast of the Greek island of Antikythera in 1901, has baffled scientists and historians for over a century. The mechanism, dating back to around 100 BCE, is a complex assembly of gears and dials housed in a wooden box dubbed the world's first analog computer.

The level of sophistication and precision of the Antikythera Mechanism is astounding, especially considering the time it was created. It is believed to have been used as an astronomical calculator, capable of predicting the positions of celestial bodies, eclipses, and even the dates of the ancient Olympic Games. The device's intricate system of gears and dials allowed its users to track the movements of the sun, moon, and planets with remarkable accuracy.

The discovery of the Antikythera Mechanism has raised numerous questions about the technological capabilities of the ancient Greeks. How could they design and construct such a complex and precise instrument over 2,000 years ago? What other advanced technologies might they have possessed that have been lost to history? The answers to these questions remain elusive, but the Antikythera Mechanism serves as a testament to the ingenuity and skill of its creators.

One of the most intriguing aspects of the Antikythera Mechanism is the mystery surrounding its purpose and use. While it is widely accepted that the device was used for astronomical calculations, some researchers have proposed alternative theories. For example, some suggest that it may have been used for astrological purposes, while others believe it could have been a teaching tool or even a form of ancient entertainment.

The Antikythera Mechanism continues to captivate the imagination of scientists, historians, and the general public alike. Its discovery has inspired a renewed interest in studying ancient technology and has led to new techniques for examining and preserving delicate artifacts. As researchers continue to study the mechanism and unlock its secrets, it serves as a powerful reminder of the incredible achievements of the ancient world and the mysteries that still await discovery.

The Baghdad Battery: A Prehistoric Power Source?

The Baghdad Battery, also known as the Parthian Battery, is a fascinating and enigmatic artifact that has puzzled historians and scientists for decades. Discovered in the 1930s near Baghdad, Iraq, this peculiar object has been the subject of much debate and speculation. Could it be evidence of an ancient and advanced civilization with knowledge of electricity, or is it simply a misunderstood relic from a bygone era?

The Baghdad Battery consists of a small clay jar, approximately five inches tall, containing a copper cylinder and an iron rod. The jar is sealed with an asphalt plug, leading some researchers to believe it may have been used to store an acidic or alkaline substance. When filled with such a substance, the combination of copper and iron could have produced a weak electrical current, similar to a modern-day battery.

The idea of an ancient battery is undoubtedly intriguing, and if proven true, it would drastically change our understanding of the technological capabilities of ancient civilizations. However, there is much debate among experts as to the true purpose of the Baghdad Battery.

Some researchers argue that the artifact was used for electroplating, a process in which a thin layer of metal is deposited onto another metal object. This theory is supported by the discovery of small gold-plated objects in the region, which could have been created using a primitive form of electroplating. Others believe that the battery may have been used for medicinal purposes, such as pain relief or treating various ailments through a process known as electrotherapy.

On the other hand, skepticism argues that the Baghdad Battery is not a battery at all. They contend the artifact is a storage vessel for sacred scrolls or other valuable items. The presence of the copper and iron components could be coincidental, and the asphalt plug may have been used to protect the contents from moisture and decay.

Despite the ongoing debate, the Baghdad Battery remains a mysterious and captivating artifact. Its true purpose may never be definitively proven, but it serves as a testament to the ingenuity and curiosity of ancient civilizations. Whether it was a prehistoric power source or a simple storage vessel, the Baghdad Battery continues to spark the imagination and inspire further research into the mysteries of our past.

The Sumerian King List: Blending Myth and History in Ancient Mesopotamia

The Sumerian King List is an ancient manuscript that records the names, reigns, and locations of the kings of Sumer. This early civilization thrived in Mesopotamia (modern-day Iraq) from around 4500 to 1900 BC. The list is a unique historical document, combining mythical and real kings, providing a fascinating glimpse into the beliefs and historical understanding of the ancient Sumerians.

The Sumerian King List is believed to have been compiled around 2100 BC during the reign of the Third Dynasty of Ur. It has been found inscribed on several clay tablets and prisms, with a complete version of the Weld-Blundell Prism, housed in the Ashmolean Museum in Oxford, England. The list is written in the Sumerian language using cuneiform script, one of the earliest known writing systems.

The list begins with the mythical antediluvian (pre-flood) kings, who are said to have ruled for incredibly long periods, ranging from 18,600 to 43,200 years. These kings are described as having descended from heaven, and their reigns are believed to have taken place in the cities of Eridu, Bad-tibira, Larak, Sippar, and Shuruppak. The list then moves on to the post-flood kings, whose reigns are recorded in more realistic timeframes, ranging from a few years to a few centuries.

One of the most intriguing aspects of the Sumerian King List is its blending of myth and history. While the antediluvian kings are mythical figures, the post-flood kings are believed to be historical rulers whose reigns can be corroborated with other sources, such as archaeological evidence and contemporary inscriptions. This combination of myth and history suggests that the ancient Sumerians viewed their past as a continuum, with the divine and human realms closely intertwined.

The Sumerian King List also provides valuable information about the political history of ancient Mesopotamia. It records the rise and fall of various city-states, such as Kish, Uruk, Ur, and Lagash, and the dynasties that ruled them. The list also mentions several important historical figures, such as Gilgamesh, the legendary hero of the Epic of Gilgamesh, and Sargon of Akkad, the founder of the Akkadian Empire.

Despite its historical significance, the Sumerian King List has its controversies. For example, some scholars have questioned the accuracy of the reign lengths, particularly for the early post-flood kings, who are said to have ruled for hundreds of years. Additionally, the list needs to be more comprehensive, as it omits certain kings and dynasties that are known from other sources. Nevertheless, the Sumerian King List remains an invaluable resource for understanding the history and culture of one of the world's earliest civilizations.

The Piri Reis Map: A Mysterious Chart of Unknown Origins

The Piri Reis Map, named after its creator, the Ottoman admiral and cartographer Piri Reis, is a fascinating and enigmatic artifact that has captured the imagination of historians, archaeologists, and conspiracy theorists alike. Created in 1513, the map is a stunningly accurate representation of the world as it was known at the time, with one significant exception: it appears to depict the coastline of Antarctica, a continent that would not be officially discovered for another three centuries.

The map, drawn on gazelle skin, is a compilation of various sources, including maps from the time of Alexander the Great, ancient Indian and Chinese charts, and even maps from the legendary lost city of Atlantis, according to Piri Reis himself. The map's remarkable accuracy and the inclusion of seemingly impossible geographical features have led to many theories attempting to explain its origins.

One of the most striking aspects of the Piri Reis Map is its depiction of the South American coastline, which is remarkably accurate for a time when cartography was still a relatively primitive science. The map also shows the Andes Mountains, which were not officially discovered until 1527. This has led some to speculate that the map was based on information from an advanced ancient civilization, perhaps even the fabled Atlantis.

However, the Piri Reis Map's most controversial aspect is its apparent depiction of Antarctica. The continent is shown as a landmass connected to South America, with a detailed coastline that closely matches the actual topography of the continent beneath its ice sheet. This has led some to suggest that the map is evidence of an advanced ancient civilization with the technology to explore and map the world's most remote regions.

Skeptics argue that the map's depiction of Antarctica is simply a coincidence or a misinterpretation of the data available to Piri Reis at the time. They point out that the map also contains numerous inaccuracies, including mythical islands and the misplacement of certain geographical features. Furthermore, they argue that the advanced technology required to create such an accurate map would have left other traces in the archaeological record which have yet to be found.

Despite these criticisms, the Piri Reis Map remains an enduring mystery that continues to captivate researchers and enthusiasts alike. Its mysterious origins and the tantalizing possibility of a connection to a lost ancient civilization ensure that the map will continue to be a subject of fascination and debate for years. However, as we dig deeper into the secrets of our past, we may unlock the true story behind this mysterious chart of unknown origins.

The Dropa Stones: Ancient Discs with an Extraterrestrial Connection?

The Dropa Stones are a collection of mysterious, ancient artifacts that have captivated the imagination of historians, archaeologists, and enthusiasts alike. These enigmatic discs, allegedly discovered in the remote mountains of China, have been the subject of much debate and speculation. Are they remnants of an ancient, advanced civilization, or do they hold evidence of extraterrestrial contact? In this section, we will delve into the intriguing story of the Dropa Stones and explore the theories surrounding their origin and purpose.

The story of the Dropa Stones began in 1938 when a Chinese archaeologist named Chi Pu Tei led an expedition to the remote Bayan Har Mountains in the Qinghai Province of China. They stumbled upon a series of caves containing a trove of ancient graves there. Inside these graves, they found the skeletal remains of a peculiar race of small-statured people with large, elongated skulls. Alongside these remains, the team discovered a collection of stone discs, each measuring about 9 inches in diameter and featuring a small hole in the center.

Upon closer examination, the discs were found to be etched with a series of tiny, intricate grooves that spiraled outwards from the center hole. When these grooves were studied under a microscope, they contained minuscule, hieroglyph-like markings. This discovery led to a frenzy of speculation, with many suggesting that the discs were ancient records left behind by a long-lost civilization.

The mystery deepened in the 1960s when a Russian scientist named Dr. Tsum Um Nui claimed to have deciphered the markings on the Dropa Stones. According to his translation, the discs told the story of a group of extraterrestrial beings called the Dropa, who crash-landed in the Bayan Har Mountains 12,000 years ago. Unable to repair their damaged spacecraft, the Dropa were stranded on Earth and eventually integrated with the local population.

This sensational claim sparked interest in the Dropa Stones, with many embracing the idea that these artifacts were evidence of ancient extraterrestrial contact. However, others have cast doubt on the authenticity of Dr. Tsum Um Nui's translation, arguing that the markings on the discs need to be bigger and more worn to be accurately deciphered.

Skepticism surrounding the Dropa Stones has only grown over the years, with some researchers questioning the very existence of the artifacts themselves. The original discs have reportedly been lost; no photographs or detailed descriptions of the stones have surfaced. This has led some to dismiss the entire story as a hoax or an elaborate myth.

Despite the controversy and uncertainty surrounding the Dropa Stones, they continue to captivate the imagination of those who are drawn to the mysteries of our ancient past. Whether relics of a forgotten civilization or evidence of extraterrestrial contact, the Dropa

Stones are a fascinating reminder of the enduring allure of unexplained artifacts.

The Shroud of Turin: A Holy Relic or a Masterful Forgery?

The Shroud of Turin is one of history's most debated and enigmatic artifacts. Believed by many to be the burial cloth of Jesus Christ, this mysterious linen cloth bears the faint image of a man who appears to have suffered physical trauma consistent with crucifixion. As a result, the shroud has been a subject of intense study, veneration, and skepticism for centuries, with experts and enthusiasts trying to determine whether it is a genuine relic or an elaborate hoax.

The first recorded mention of the Shroud of Turin dates back to the 14th century when it was displayed in a church in Lirey, France. The shroud eventually made its way to Turin, Italy, in 1578, where it has been housed in the Cathedral of Saint John the Baptist ever since. Over the years, the shroud has been subjected to numerous scientific tests and examinations to determine its authenticity.

One of the most significant investigations into the shroud was the radiocarbon dating test conducted in 1988. Three separate laboratories analyzed the cloth samples and concluded that they originated between 1260 and 1390 AD, suggesting that the shroud was likely a medieval forgery. However, subsequent research has cast doubt on these findings, with some scientists arguing that the samples tested were contaminated by fibers from later repairs to the cloth.

In addition to the radiocarbon dating controversy, various other aspects of the shroud have been scrutinized, including the bloodstains, the image formation, and the historical record. Some researchers have proposed that the image on the shroud was created using a primitive form of photography. In contrast, others believe it may have resulted from a natural chemical reaction. The bloodstains on the cloth have also been analyzed, with some experts claiming that they are consistent with the wounds inflicted upon Jesus during his crucifixion, while others argue that the stains are too perfect and were likely painted on.

The historical record surrounding the shroud is equally puzzling.

While there is no definitive proof that the Shroud of Turin existed before the 14th century, some scholars have suggested that it may have been the same cloth mentioned in the Bible and other early Christian texts. However, the lack of concrete evidence has left this theory open to debate.

Ultimately, whether the Shroud of Turin is a genuine holy relic or a masterful forgery still needs to be answered. Despite the numerous scientific tests and historical investigations, the shroud continues to captivate and mystify researchers, believers, and skeptics alike. As with many unexplained artifacts, the allure of the Shroud of Turin lies in the tantalizing possibility that it could provide a tangible connection to one of the most significant events in human history. However, until definitive proof is found, the debate over the shroud's authenticity will continue to rage on, serving as a testament to the enduring fascination with the unknown.

The Crystal Skulls: Enigmatic Carvings with a Mysterious Purpose

The Crystal Skulls are a collection of enigmatic artifacts that have captivated the imagination of historians, archaeologists, and enthusiasts alike. These intricately carved objects, made from clear or milky quartz crystal, are shaped to resemble human skulls. Yet, the origins of these mysterious artifacts remain mysterious, with theories ranging from ancient civilizations to extraterrestrial influences.

The most famous of these artifacts is the Mitchell-Hedges Skull, discovered in 1924 by British adventurer Frederick Mitchell-Hedges and his daughter Anna during an expedition in Belize. The skull, made of clear quartz crystal and roughly life-sized, is renowned for its remarkable craftsmanship and near-perfect anatomical accuracy. The skull's jaw is detachable, and the entire piece is carved from a single crystal block.

The enigma surrounding the Crystal Skulls is not limited to their origin. The methods used to create these artifacts have also been debated among experts. Given the hardness of quartz crystals and the lack of advanced tools available to ancient civilizations, it is still being determined how these skulls were carved with such precision. Some researchers have suggested that the skulls were crafted using primitive tools and techniques. In contrast, others argue that the level of detail and accuracy in the carvings could only have been achieved with advanced technology, possibly from an extraterrestrial source.

The purpose of the Crystal Skulls is another aspect that has puzzled researchers. Some theories suggest that these artifacts were used for religious or ceremonial purposes. In contrast, others believe they may have served as tools for healing or even as a means of communication with the spirit world. The skulls have also been linked to the legend of the lost continent of Atlantis, with some speculating that they were created by the advanced civilization that once inhabited the mythical land.

The authenticity of the Crystal Skulls has been a subject of controversy as well. Many experts believe that some, if not all, of the skulls are modern forgeries created in the 19th or 20th centuries. This skepticism is fueled by the fact that no crystal skulls have been found in a documented archaeological context, and many of the skulls have been traced back to known forgers or dubious sources.

Despite the questions surrounding their origins, methods of creation, and purpose, the Crystal Skulls continue to fascinate and intrigue those who encounter them. These enigmatic artifacts remind us of the enduring allure of unexplained mysteries and the human desire to uncover the secrets of our past. As researchers continue to study the Crystal Skulls, we may unlock the truth behind these fascinating relics and their mysteries.

The Saqqara Bird: Unraveling the Mystery of an Ancient Egyptian Enigma

The Saqqara Bird is a fascinating and enigmatic artifact discovered in 1898 during excavations at the Saqqara necropolis near Memphis in Egypt. This small wooden object, dating back to around 200 BC during the Ptolemaic period, has generated much debate and speculation among historians, archaeologists, and enthusiasts due to its unique design and possible implications.

Measuring approximately 7 inches (18 cm) in length and 5.5 inches (14 cm) in height, the Saqqara Bird is carved from sycamore wood and resembles a bird or a glider with carefully crafted wings, a tail, and a head with prominent eyes. The artifact is relatively well-preserved, considering its age, although some parts have been damaged or lost over time.

The purpose and significance of the Saqqara Bird have been the subject of much debate. Some researchers have suggested that the artifact could represent evidence of ancient aviation technology or an understanding of aerodynamics. In addition, the design of the wings, tail, and head might indicate that the ancient Egyptians had knowledge of flight principles and possibly even experimented with gliders or other flying devices.

Proponents of this theory point to the Saqqara Bird's wings being set at a dihedral angle, a feature found in modern aircraft to provide stability during flight. Additionally, the artifact's tail is designed to resemble a modern aircraft's vertical stabilizer, which helps maintain directional stability.

However, many experts in Egyptology and archaeology argue that the Saqqara Bird is simply a decorative object or a child's toy and that its resemblance to modern aircraft is purely coincidental. Furthermore, they contend that no concrete evidence supports the idea that the ancient Egyptians possessed advanced knowledge of aerodynamics or flight technology.

Skeptics also point out that the Saqqara Bird lacks several crucial features necessary for flight, such as propulsion and control surfaces to maneuver the craft. Furthermore, no other artifacts or records have been found to suggest that the ancient Egyptians experimented with flight or possessed advanced aviation technology.

In conclusion, the Saqqara Bird remains an intriguing and enigmatic artifact that has captured the imagination of many. While its true purpose and significance may never be definitively proven, it serves as a testament to the ancient Egyptians' remarkable craftsmanship and artistic skill. It continues to inspire curiosity and debate among scholars and enthusiasts alike.

The Ica Stones: Controversial Depictions of Prehistoric Life

The Ica Stones are a collection of thousands of engraved stones that have sparked intense debate and controversy among historians, archaeologists, and enthusiasts of unexplained mysteries. Discovered in the Ica region of Peru, these stones depict a wide range of scenes, from everyday life to highly advanced medical procedures. What makes these stones so enigmatic is that they portray events and knowledge that should have been impossible for the ancient civilizations of the time to possess.

The Ica Stones first gained widespread attention in the 1960s when a local farmer named Basilio Uschuya claimed to have found them in a cave near the Ocucaje Desert. The stones vary in size, with some as small as a pebble and others as large as a basketball. They are composed of andesite, a volcanic rock, and feature intricate carvings that have been etched into their surface with remarkable precision.

The images on the stones are astounding, as they depict scenes that defy the conventional understanding of prehistoric life. For example, some stones show humans interacting with dinosaurs, suggesting that these two species coexisted, contrary to the widely accepted belief that dinosaurs went extinct millions of years before humans appeared on Earth. Other stones depict advanced medical procedures, such as heart and brain surgeries, and the use of telescopes and other sophisticated technology.

The authenticity of the Ica Stones has been a subject of heated debate among experts. Some argue that the stones are genuine artifacts from an ancient civilization with advanced knowledge, while others dismiss them as elaborate hoaxes. Critics point to the need for concrete evidence linking the stones to a specific time period or culture and the fact that no similar artifacts have been found in the region.

In the 1970s, Basilio Uschuya admitted to creating some of the stones himself, using images from comic books and magazines as inspiration. This confession has led many to dismiss the entire collection as a fraud. However, Uschuya later recanted his confession, claiming he only admitted to creating the stones to avoid legal trouble for selling Peruvian artifacts.

Despite the controversy surrounding their authenticity, the Ica Stones continue to captivate the imagination of those who encounter them. Moreover, they serve as a reminder that the history of our planet is filled with mysteries yet to be unraveled and that the line between fact and fiction can sometimes be blurred. Whether genuine artifacts or elaborate hoaxes, the Ica Stones undeniably hold a unique place in unexplained mysteries.

The Baltic Sea Anomaly: A Mysterious Underwater Formation

The Baltic Sea Anomaly is a captivating underwater enigma that has puzzled researchers and enthusiasts alike since its discovery in 2011. This peculiar formation, located at the bottom of the Baltic Sea between Sweden and Finland, was first detected by the Ocean X Team, a group of Swedish treasure hunters led by Peter Lindberg and Dennis Åsberg. While searching for sunken treasures, the team stumbled upon a strange, circular object on the sea floor, which appeared, unlike anything they had ever seen.

Measuring approximately 60 meters in diameter, the Baltic Sea Anomaly resembles the iconic Millennium Falcon from the Star Wars franchise. The object rests on a pillar-like structure, which raises it about 4 meters above the seabed. Surrounding the formation is a series of peculiar, angular indentations that have led some to speculate that the anomaly might be a remnant of an ancient, unknown civilization.

One of the most intriguing aspects of the Baltic Sea Anomaly is that it interferes with electronic equipment. The Ocean X Team reported that their cameras and satellite phones would malfunction whenever they approached the object, only to return to normal once they moved away. This has fueled speculation that the anomaly might be composed of materials with unusual electromagnetic properties or even that it could be an extraterrestrial artifact.

Despite the many theories surrounding the Baltic Sea Anomaly, no concrete evidence has been found to support any of them. Instead, some researchers argue that the formation is simply a natural geological occurrence, such as a glacial deposit or a volcanic rock formation. Others, however, remain convinced that the anomaly is a remnant of a lost civilization or a crashed UFO.

Several expeditions have been conducted to study the anomaly up close to unravel the mystery. Divers have collected samples from the site, and sonar scans have been performed to create detailed images of the object. However, these efforts have only deepened the enigma, as the results have been inconclusive and open to interpretation.

The Baltic Sea Anomaly continues to be a source of fascination and debate among researchers, historians, and UFO enthusiasts. Its enigmatic nature and the lack of definitive answers have only served to heighten its allure, making it one of the most captivating unexplained mysteries of our time. As we continue to explore the depths of our oceans and uncover their secrets, the Baltic Sea Anomaly stands as a testament to the enduring appeal of the unknown and the human desire to seek answers to the mysteries surrounding us.

The Enduring Allure of Unexplained Artifacts

Throughout history, humankind has been captivated by the enigma of unexplained artifacts. These mysterious objects and discoveries, seemingly out-of-place and out-of-time, challenge our understanding of the past and present and invite us to question the boundaries of our knowledge. As we have explored in this chapter, the allure of these artifacts lies in their ability to spark our curiosity, ignite our imagination, and inspire us to delve deeper into the unknown.

The Antikythera Mechanism, the Baghdad Battery, the Voynich Manuscript, and other artifacts discussed in this chapter are potent reminders of human history's vast and complex tapestry. They represent the ingenuity, creativity, and resilience of our ancestors, who, like us, sought to make sense of the world around them and unlock the secrets of the universe. Yet, these artifacts also highlight the limitations of our current understanding as they continue to defy explanation and elude categorization.

The enduring allure of unexplained artifacts is rooted in their enigmatic nature and the stories and legends surrounding them. From the extraterrestrial connections of the Dropa Stones to the religious significance of the Shroud of Turin, these artifacts have captured the hearts and minds of countless individuals, transcending cultural, religious, and geographical boundaries. They have become symbols of our collective quest for knowledge and understanding and have inspired countless works of art, literature, and scientific inquiry.

As we continue to uncover new artifacts and delve deeper into the mysteries of the past, it is essential to approach these discoveries with an open mind and a healthy dose of skepticism. While it is tempting to attribute supernatural or otherworldly origins to these enigmatic objects, it is crucial to remember that extraordinary claims require extraordinary evidence. Nevertheless, by applying rigorous scientific methods and critical thinking, we can unravel the secrets of these artifacts and, in doing so, expand our understanding of the world and our place in it.

In conclusion, the enduring allure of unexplained artifacts lies in their ability to challenge our perceptions, ignite our curiosity, and inspire us to seek answers to the unknown. As we continue to explore our past and present mysteries, these artifacts are potent reminders of the boundless potential of human curiosity and the enduring quest for knowledge. May we continue to be captivated by the enigma of unexplained artifacts, and may they inspire us to push the boundaries of our understanding as we journey together into the unknown.

9

ENIGMATIC CODES AND CIPHERS:
THE UNBREAKABLE MESSAGES

Enigmatic Codes and Ciphers

T hroughout history, humans have been fascinated by the unknown, the unexplained, and the mysterious. One area that has captured the imagination of countless individuals is the realm of unsolved codes and ciphers. These enigmatic messages, often shrouded in secrecy and intrigue, have been used for various purposes – from concealing sensitive information to taunting authorities and even hiding treasures. The allure of these cryptic communications lies in the challenge they present and the tantalizing possibility of uncovering long-lost secrets and solving age-old mysteries.

Unsolved codes and ciphers have a unique ability to captivate our attention and spark our curiosity. They represent a perfect blend of intellectual challenge and human drama, often involving stories of espionage, crime, and hidden knowledge. Decoding these messages can be likened to a thrilling treasure hunt, where each breakthrough brings us one step closer to unearthing the truth. Moreover, the fact that some of these codes have remained unsolved for centuries only adds to their mystique, as it suggests that they may contain information that is still relevant and valuable today.

The appeal of unsolved codes and ciphers also lies in their inherent complexity and the intellectual prowess required to decipher them. These messages often employ sophisticated techniques and intricate patterns, which can be awe-inspiring and humbling. Cracking a code requires creativity, logic, and perseverance, making it a deeply satisfying endeavor for those up to the challenge. Furthermore, studying these enigmatic messages can provide valuable insights into the history of cryptography and the evolution of human communication.

This chapter will delve into the fascinating world of enigmatic codes and ciphers, exploring ten of the most intriguing and unbreakable messages known to man. From the mysterious Beale ciphers to the chilling ciphers of the Zodiac Killer, these cases represent some of the most captivating and perplexing puzzles in the history of cryptography. As we journey through these remarkable stories, we will gain a deeper appreciation for the art and science of codebreaking and understand the enduring fascination with the unexplained mysteries that continue to captivate our imagination.

The Chaocipher: A Century-Old Enigma of Mechanical Cryptography

The Chaocipher, a mechanical encryption device invented by John F. Byrne in 1918, has intrigued cryptographers and codebreakers for over a century. The device's unique design and complex substitution cipher have made it one of the most enigmatic codes in the history of cryptography.

Byrne, an Irish-American writer and friend of James Joyce, created the Chaocipher to securely encrypt messages during a time when cryptography was becoming increasingly important due to World War I. The device consists of two rotating disks, each containing 26 letters of the alphabet. As the disks rotate, they create a constantly changing substitution cipher, making it incredibly difficult to crack without knowing the device's inner workings.

The Chaocipher remained shrouded in mystery for decades, as Byrne refused to reveal the principles behind his invention. He even challenged the U.S. government to crack the code, offering a cash reward to anyone who could decipher a series of encrypted messages. However, despite numerous attempts by skilled codebreakers, the Chaocipher's secrets remained hidden.

It wasn't until 2010, long after Byrne's death, that the principles behind the Chaocipher were finally revealed. Moshe Rubin, an Israeli researcher, discovered a detailed description of the device in Byrne's personal papers, donated to the National Cryptologic Museum in Maryland. With this newfound knowledge, Rubin could construct a working replica of the Chaocipher and demonstrate its encryption process.

Although the principles behind the Chaocipher are now understood, many of its encrypted messages remain unsolved. Moreover, the device's complex substitution cipher continues to challenge cryptographers, ensuring that the Chaocipher remains a fascinating enigma in the world of cryptography.

The Zodiac Killer's Ciphers: Taunting the Police and Public

The Zodiac Killer, one of the most notorious and enigmatic serial killers in American history, terrorized the San Francisco Bay Area during the late 1960s and early 1970s. Responsible for at least five brutal murders, the Zodiac Killer was never caught or conclusively identified. What sets this case apart from other mysteries is the killer's penchant for sending taunting letters and cryptic messages to the police and media, which included a series of complex ciphers that have baffled experts for decades.

The first of these ciphers, the 408 Cipher, was sent in three separate parts to three different newspapers in the Bay Area in 1969. The killer demanded that the newspapers publish the ciphers on their front pages, or he would go on a killing spree. The newspapers complied, and the ciphers were published. Amateur codebreakers Donald and Bettye Harden cracked the 408 Cipher, revealing a chilling message in which the Zodiac Killer claimed to be collecting "slaves for the afterlife" through his murders.

However, the Zodiac Killer's subsequent ciphers have remained unsolved. The most famous is the 340 Cipher, sent to the San Francisco Chronicle in November 1969. Despite the efforts of countless amateur and professional cryptanalysts, the 340 Cipher has never been conclusively deciphered. Some believe the cipher contains the Zodiac Killer's true identity, while others think it may be another disturbing message about his motives or plans.

Another intriguing cipher associated with the Zodiac Killer is the 13-character "My Name Is" cipher, included in a letter sent to the San Francisco Chronicle in April 1970. The killer claimed his name was hidden within the cipher, but despite numerous attempts to crack the code, his identity remains a mystery.

The unsolved ciphers of the Zodiac Killer continue to captivate the public's imagination, as they represent a compelling challenge for codebreakers and a chilling reminder of the killer's twisted mind. The fact that the Zodiac Killer was never caught only adds to the allure of these enigmatic messages, as the possibility remains that the key to unlocking the killer's identity lies hidden within the ciphers, waiting for someone to decipher them finally.

As we investigate further into the world of unexplained codes and ciphers, the Zodiac Killer's messages stand out as a prime example of how these cryptic communications can both fascinate and frustrate those who attempt to unravel their secrets. The mystery of the Zodiac Killer's ciphers is a testament to the power of unsolved codes to captivate our collective imagination and challenge our intellect, even decades after they were first created.

The Beale Ciphers: A Hidden Treasure Waiting to be Unearthed

The Beale Ciphers, a series of three encrypted texts, have captured the imagination of treasure hunters and cryptographers for almost two centuries. These mysterious ciphers allegedly hold the key to a hidden treasure worth millions of dollars buried somewhere in the United States. The story of the Beale Ciphers is a tale of adventure, intrigue, and an unyielding quest for fortune that has yet to be discovered.

The story begins in 1817 when Thomas J. Beale allegedly discovered a vast treasure while on a hunting expedition in the Rocky Mountains. The treasure, consisting of gold, silver, and precious gems, was said to be worth millions of dollars. Beale, fearing that the treasure would be lost or stolen, buried it in a secret location and created a set of ciphers that would reveal its whereabouts.

Beale entrusted a box containing the ciphers to a friend, Robert Morriss, with instructions to open it if Beale did not return within ten years. When Beale failed to reappear, Morriss opened the box and discovered three encrypted messages. The first cipher supposedly described the exact location of the treasure, the second detailed the contents of the treasure, and the third revealed the names and contact information of Beale's associates who were to inherit the fortune.

Over the years, numerous attempts have been made to crack the

Beale Ciphers, but only the second cipher has been successfully decrypted. Using the United States Declaration of Independence as a key, the second cipher revealed a description of the treasure, further fueling the obsession to uncover the hidden fortune. However, the first and third ciphers have remained unsolved, leaving the exact location of the treasure and the identities of Beale's associates a mystery.

The Beale Ciphers have attracted countless treasure hunters, cryptographers, and enthusiasts who have spent years trying to unlock the secrets of the remaining ciphers. Some believe the treasure is buried in Bedford County, Virginia, while others argue that the story is a hoax and the ciphers are nothing more than an elaborate ruse. Despite the skepticism, the allure of the Beale Ciphers and the possibility of unearthing a hidden fortune continue to captivate the minds of many.

The Beale Ciphers is a testament to the enduring fascination with unexplained codes and ciphers. Whether the treasure is real or a figment of imagination, the quest to solve the enigmatic messages has become a treasure hunt. As long as the ciphers remain unsolved, the legend of the Beale treasure will continue to inspire generations of treasure hunters, cryptographers, and mystery enthusiasts, all seeking to uncover the truth behind the unbreakable messages.

The Dorabella Cipher: Elgar's Enigmatic Message

The world of unsolved codes and ciphers is not limited to criminal cases and ancient artifacts. Sometimes, the most intriguing mysteries can be found in the personal correspondence of famous individuals. One such enigma is the Dorabella Cipher, a cryptic message penned by the renowned English composer Sir Edward Elgar.

In July 1897, Elgar sent a peculiar note to his close friend Dora Penny, affectionately known as "Dorabella." The message consisted of 87 characters arranged in three lines, with each character resembling a series of semi-circles oriented in different directions. The note was accompanied by a conventional letter, but the contents of the cipher have remained a mystery for over a century.

Many attempts have been made to decode the Dorabella Cipher, but they have yet to produce a universally accepted solution. Some experts believe the message is a simple substitution cipher, where each character represents a letter of the alphabet. Others have suggested that the semi-circular symbols may represent musical notes, given Elgar's profession as a composer. However, despite numerous efforts, a definitive decryption has yet to be achieved.

Several factors contribute to the enigmatic nature of the Dorabella Cipher. Firstly, the cipher's unique symbols and arrangement make it challenging to determine the underlying structure of the message. Additionally, the lack of context and the absence of any known code-book or key make it challenging to verify the accuracy of any proposed solutions.

The relationship between Elgar and Dora Penny adds another layer of intrigue to the mystery. The two were known to share a close bond, and it has been speculated that the cipher may contain a personal message or even a declaration of love. However, without successful decryption, the true nature of the message remains a matter of conjecture.

The Dorabella Cipher is a fascinating example of the enduring appeal of unexplained codes and ciphers. It demonstrates that even in personal correspondence, the allure of a hidden message can captivate the imagination and inspire countless attempts at decryption. As with many of the enigmas discussed in this chapter, the Dorabella Cipher continues to challenge and intrigue experts and enthusiasts, ensuring its place in the pantheon of unbreakable codes.

The Kryptos Sculpture: A Puzzle in Plain Sight

The Kryptos Sculpture, an enigmatic piece of art that has captivated codebreakers and enthusiasts for decades, is a testament to the enduring allure of unsolved codes and ciphers. Located in the court-yard of the Central Intelligence Agency (C.I.A.) headquarters in Langley, Virginia, the Kryptos Sculpture is a fascinating paradox: a puzzle hidden in plain sight yet shrouded in secrecy.

Created by American artist Jim Sanborn in 1990, the Kryptos Sculpture is a 12-foot-tall, S-shaped copper scroll adorned with 1,735 characters, including letters, numbers, and question marks. The text is divided into four sections, each containing an encrypted message. The sculpture's name, Kryptos, is derived from the Greek word for "hidden," reflecting the enigmatic nature of the codes inscribed on its surface.

The first three sections of the Kryptos Sculpture have been successfully deciphered, revealing messages that touch upon themes of discovery, exploration, and the limits of human knowledge. The first section, for example, contains a poetic phrase that reads, "Between subtle shading and the absence of light lies the nuance of iqlusion." The second section quotes the diary of archaeologist Howard Carter, describing the moment he discovered the tomb of Tutankhamun. Finally, the third section is a paraphrased excerpt from a classified document discussing gathering intelligence through satellite imagery.

However, the fourth and final section of the Kryptos Sculpture still needs to be solved, despite the efforts of countless amateur and professional codebreakers. This 97-character sequence has stumped even the brightest minds at the C.I.A. and the National Security Agency (N.S.A.), who have held internal competitions to crack the code. The artist, Jim Sanborn, has provided two clues to aid in deciphering the message: the words "Berlin" and "clock." Yet, these hints have only deepened the sculpture's mystery, as they raise more questions than they answer.

The Kryptos Sculpture symbolizes the human desire to uncover hidden truths and solve the seemingly unsolvable. As long as the fourth section remains undeciphered, the sculpture will continue to intrigue and challenge those who encounter it, inviting them to unlock its secrets and join the ranks of history's greatest codebreakers. In this way, the Kryptos Sculpture embodies the spirit of enigmatic codes and ciphers, demonstrating that even in an age of advanced technology and sophisticated algorithms, some puzzles remain beyond our grasp.

The Phaistos Disk: An Ancient Enigma from Crete

The Phaistos Disk is one of the most enigmatic artifacts ever discovered, leaving historians and cryptographers baffled for over a century.

Unearthed in 1908 by Italian archaeologist Luigi Pernier at the Minoan palace of Phaistos on the island of Crete, this small, circular clay disk has become an enduring mystery that continues to captivate researchers and enthusiasts alike.

Measuring approximately 16 centimeters in diameter and dating back to the second millennium B.C.E., the Phaistos Disk is adorned with 241 mysterious symbols pressed into the clay while still soft. These symbols, arranged in a spiral pattern, depict various objects, animals, and human figures. What makes the Phaistos Disk so intriguing is that the symbols appear to be part of an unknown writing system that has never been seen before or since.

Despite numerous attempts to decipher the disk, a definitive interpretation has yet to be agreed upon. Some scholars believe that the symbols represent a hieroglyphic script, while others argue that they are a syllabic or alphabetic writing system. Some even speculate that the disk may be a forgery created to deceive and confound the academic community.

One of the most popular theories is that the Phaistos Disk is a religious or ritual object, possibly used for divination or as a calendar. This theory is supported by symbols representing celestial bodies, such as the sun and the moon. However, this theory still needs a Rosetta Stone-like artifact to provide the key to understanding the symbols.

Another fascinating aspect of the Phaistos Disk is the method used to create the symbols. Each symbol was pressed into the clay using a set of small, individual stamps, making it one of the earliest known examples of movable type. This innovative technique suggests that the Minoan civilization was far more advanced than previously believed, adding another layer of intrigue to the enigma of the Phaistos Disk.

As with many unexplained mysteries, the Phaistos Disk has inspired countless amateur sleuths and cryptographers to try deciphering its secrets. Unfortunately, while some claim to have cracked the code, no universally accepted solution has emerged, leaving the true meaning of the disk shrouded in mystery.

The Phaistos Disk is a powerful reminder of the limits of our knowledge and understanding of ancient civilizations. Yet, despite our best efforts, this enigmatic artifact continues to elude explanation, captivating the imagination of scholars and enthusiasts alike. As we search for answers, the Phaistos Disk remains a tantalizing puzzle, inviting us to unlock the secrets of a long-lost world.

The Shugborough Inscription: A Mysterious Message on a Monument

Nestled within the picturesque grounds of Shugborough Hall in Staffordshire, England, lies an enigmatic monument that has puzzled historians, codebreakers, and enthusiasts for centuries. Known as the Shepherd's Monument, this 18th-century sculpture features a curious inscription that has remained undeciphered to this day. As a result, the Shugborough Inscription, as it is commonly referred to, has captivated the minds of many, sparking numerous theories and speculations about its meaning and origin.

The Shepherd's Monument, commissioned by Thomas Anson and completed in 1748, is a peculiar structure that features a relief of Nicolas Poussin's painting, "The Shepherds of Arcadia." The painting depicts a group of shepherds gathered around a tomb, inscribed with the Latin phrase "Et in Arcadia ego," meaning "Even in Arcadia, I am." This phrase is often interpreted as a reminder of the presence of death, even in idyllic settings. However, the inscription below the relief has garnered the most attention and intrigue.

Carved into the monument are the capital letters "O.U.O.S. V.A.V.V." followed by the letter "D" on a separate line. The meaning of this cryptic sequence has eluded experts for centuries, with many attempting to decipher its hidden message. Some believe it to be a coded message, while others speculate it may be an acronym or an abbreviation of a Latin phrase. Unfortunately, despite numerous attempts, no one has been able to provide a definitive explanation for the Shugborough Inscription.

Over the years, various theories have emerged regarding the purpose and meaning of the inscription. Some believe it to be a tribute to a deceased loved one, while others suggest it may hold the key to the location of the fabled Holy Grail. One popular theory posits that the inscription is a message left by the Knights Templar, a medieval Christian military order rumored to have discovered hidden treasures and relics during their time in the Holy Land.

Another intriguing theory is that the inscription is a cipher created by the 18th-century polymath Sir Isaac Newton, who is known to have dabbled in cryptography. This theory is supported by the fact that Thomas Anson, the commissioner of the monument, was a member of the Royal Society, an organization to which Newton also belonged. However, like all other theories, this still needs to be proven.

The Shugborough Inscription continues to be a source of fascination and debate among historians, codebreakers, and enthusiasts alike. Its enigmatic nature has inspired countless attempts at decipherment, yet it remains one of the world's most enduring unexplained mysteries. The inscription is a testament to the allure of the unknown and the human desire to uncover hidden truths, even in the face of seemingly insurmountable challenges. As long as the Shugborough Inscription remains undeciphered, it will continue to captivate the imaginations of those who encounter it, inviting them to ponder its mysterious origins and elusive meaning.

The Tamam Shud Case: A Dead Man's Unbreakable Code

The Tamam Shud case, also known as the "Mystery of the Somerton Man," is a perplexing unsolved case that has captivated the imagination of codebreakers, amateur sleuths, and the general public for over seven decades. It is a tale shrouded in enigma, involving an unidentified corpse, a cryptic message, and an unbreakable code that baffles experts today.

On December 1, 1948, the body of an unknown man was discovered on Somerton Beach near Adelaide, South Australia. The man was well-dressed, clean-shaven, and appeared in his early 40s. Despite an extensive investigation, authorities could not determine his identity or the cause of his death. The only clue found on the body was a small scrap of paper hidden in a secret pocket of the man's pants, which bore the words "Tamam Shud," meaning "ended" or "finished" in Persian.

As the investigation continued, a mysterious brown suitcase was discovered in a nearby train station's luggage room, believed to belong to the unidentified man. The suitcase contained a small, tightly rolled piece of paper with a series of seemingly random letters arranged in five lines. This cryptic message, referred to as the "Somerton Man Code," has never been deciphered, despite the efforts of numerous codebreakers and cryptanalysts over the years.

The Tamam Shud case has generated countless theories and speculations, ranging from the man being a Cold War spy to a victim of a love affair gone wrong. Some believe that the code may hold the key to the man's identity or provide clues to his death's circumstances. Others argue that the message may be a red herring to distract and confuse investigators.

Despite time and technological advancements, the Tamam Shud case remains unsolved, and the Somerton Man's identity and the meaning behind the mysterious code continue to elude experts. This enduring enigma is a testament to the human fascination with the unknown and the allure of unexplained codes and ciphers. As long as the code remains unbroken, the mystery of the Somerton Man will continue to captivate the imagination of those who seek to unravel its secrets.

The Ricky McCormick Notes: Cryptic Clues in a Murder Case

In June 1999, the body of 41-year-old Ricky McCormick was discovered in a remote field in St. Charles County, Missouri. The case was puzzling from the start, as McCormick had no known connection to the area and no apparent reason to be there. However, the most enigmatic aspect of the case was the discovery of two cryptic notes in McCormick's pockets, which have baffled investigators and codebreakers for over two decades.

The notes, written on two separate pieces of paper, were a jumble of letters, numbers, and symbols that defy any logical explanation. Yet, despite extensive efforts by the F.B.I.'s Cryptanalysis and Racketeering Records Unit (C.R.R.U.) and numerous amateur codebreakers, the meaning behind McCormick's mysterious notes remains a closely guarded secret.

One theory suggests that the notes may be a form of shorthand or personal code that only McCormick himself could understand. This idea is supported by the fact that McCormick was known to have a history of writing cryptic messages, even as a child. However, the complexity of the notes and the fact that they were found on his person at the time of his death suggest that they may hold more significance than mere personal musings.

Another possibility is that the notes are related to criminal activity. McCormick had a troubled past, with a history of drug use and petty crime. Therefore, some speculate that the notes may be a form of coded communication between McCormick and other criminals, possibly containing information about drug deals or other illicit activities. However, this theory has not been substantiated, and the contents of the notes remain a mystery.

The Ricky McCormick case is a prime example of how unexplained codes and ciphers can add more intrigue to an already baffling mystery. The fact that the notes have remained unsolved for over two decades only adds to their enigmatic allure. As with many of the other mysteries discussed in this chapter, the Ricky McCormick notes serve as a reminder that there are still secrets waiting to be uncovered and that the world of codes and ciphers is far from being fully understood.

The D'Agapeyeff Cipher: A Challenge from a Cryptographer

The D'Agapeyeff Cipher stands out as a particularly intriguing puzzle in the world of enigmatic codes and ciphers. This cipher was created by Alexander D'Agapeyeff, a Russian-born British cryptographer, cartographer, and author. In 1939, D'Agapeyeff published a book titled "Codes and Ciphers," which aimed to teach readers the basics of cryptography. As a challenge to his readers, D'Agapeyeff included an encrypted message at the end of the book, inviting them to decipher it. Little did he know that this seemingly simple challenge would remain unsolved for decades, capturing the imagination of cryptanalysts and enthusiasts alike.

The D'Agapeyeff Cipher consists of numbers arranged in five columns and twenty rows. Each number is two or three digits long, and the entire message contains 180 digits. The cipher has proven incredibly difficult to crack despite its seemingly simple appearance. Over the years, numerous attempts have been made to decipher the message, but they have yet to be successful.

One of the reasons the D'Agapeyeff Cipher has remained unsolved is the need for more context or clues surrounding the message. Unlike famous ciphers, such as the Zodiac Killer's ciphers, there is no accompanying plaintext or known subject matter to help guide would-be solvers. Additionally, D'Agapeyeff claimed to have forgotten his method to encrypt the message, making it even more challenging to decipher.

The D'Agapeyeff Cipher has attracted the attention of both amateur and professional cryptanalysts, who have proposed various theories and methods for breaking the code. Some have suggested that the cipher is a polyalphabetic substitution, while others believe it may be a transposition cipher. There have also been suggestions that the cipher is, in fact, a hoax or an unsolvable puzzle created by D'Agapeyeff to confound and frustrate his readers.

Despite numerous attempts and theories, the D'Agapeyeff Cipher remains one of the most famous unsolved codes in the world of cryptography. Its mystery has only heightened its allure, inspiring generations of codebreakers to take up the challenge. As with many of the other unexplained codes and ciphers discussed in this chapter, the D'Agapeyeff Cipher is a testament to the human fascination with the unknown and the desire to uncover hidden secrets. Whether or not the cipher will ever be solved remains to be seen, but its enigmatic nature ensures that it will continue to captivate the minds of cryptographers and enthusiasts for years to come.

The Enduring Fascination with Unexplained Codes and Ciphers

Throughout history, the allure of unsolved codes and ciphers has captivated the minds of scholars, cryptographers, and laypeople. The enigmatic messages explored in this chapter testify to the human desire for secrecy, mystery, and the thrill of the unknown. Each of these cases, from the ancient Phaistos Disk to the modern-day Kryptos Sculpture, offers a unique glimpse into the minds of their creators and the societies in which they lived.

The fascination with unexplained codes and ciphers is not merely an intellectual exercise or a hobby for armchair detectives. Instead, it reflects our innate curiosity and drive to uncover hidden truths. These mysterious messages challenge our intellect, spark our imagination, and invite us to delve deeper into history, language, and cryptography.

Moreover, studying these enigmatic codes and ciphers can have practical applications in cryptography and computer science. By attempting to crack these unsolved messages, researchers can develop new techniques and algorithms that may be useful in modern encryption and data security. In this sense, pursuing these ancient and historical mysteries can contribute to advancing contemporary technology.

As we continue to explore the world of unexplained codes and ciphers, we are reminded that much remains to be discovered. Yet, with each discovery, we gain a greater appreciation for the ingenuity and creativity of those who have come before us. And as we strive to unlock the secrets of these enigmatic messages, we are also unlocking a deeper understanding of ourselves and our shared human history.

In conclusion, the enduring fascination with unexplained codes and ciphers is a testament to the power of mystery and the human desire to uncover hidden truths. As we continue to unravel these cryptic messages, we gain insight into the past and contribute to developing new technologies and methods for the future. The world of unexplained codes and ciphers is a rich and intriguing landscape that will continue to captivate our imaginations and challenge our intellect for generations to come.

10

STRANGE COINCIDENCES AND SYNCHRONICITIES: THE PATTERNS OF FATE

Strange Coincidences and Synchronicities

Have you ever experienced a moment when a seemingly random event or circumstance suddenly becomes more profound and meaningful? Perhaps you've bumped into an old friend in a foreign country or discovered that you share a birthday with someone you've just met. These strange coincidences and synchronicities can leave us awestruck as if the universe is conspiring to bring about these unlikely connections.

Coincidences and synchronicities are fascinating phenomena that have captured the imagination of countless individuals throughout history. They challenge our understanding of the world and force us to question whether there is more to life than meets the eye. Are these events merely the result of chance and probability, or do they hint at a hidden order underlying the fabric of reality?

In this chapter, we will delve into the mysterious realm of coincidences and synchronicities, exploring everything from the twin tragedy of the Jim Twins to the three Napoleon coincidences. We will also examine famous historical coincidences, such as the eerie similarities between the lives of Abraham Lincoln and John F. Kennedy.

As we embark on this journey, it is important to remember that the true nature of coincidences and synchronicities may never be fully understood. However, by examining these phenomena from various perspectives, we can better appreciate the mystery and wonder of life's unexplained patterns. So let's open our minds and embrace the possibility that there may be more to these strange occurrences than mere chance and that they may be the universe's way of revealing the interconnectedness of all things.

The Twin Tragedy of the Jim Twins: A Tale of Extraordinary Coincidences

In the annals of strange coincidences and synchronicities, few stories are as remarkable as that of the Jim Twins. Born on April 28, 1940, in Ohio, Jim Lewis and Jim Springer were identical twins separated at birth and adopted by different families. Unbeknownst to each other, they would go on to lead eerily parallel lives, only to be reunited 39 years later in a twist of fate that would leave the world in awe.

The twins were separated when they were only three weeks old, as their biological mother could not care for them. The Lewis family adopted Jim Lewis, while the Springers adopted Jim Springer. The two families had no contact, and the boys grew up without knowing their twin brother's existence.

As the years passed, the Jim Twins led strikingly similar lives. Both were named James by their adoptive parents and married women named Linda. When their first marriages ended in divorce, they each went on to marry women named Betty. Remarkably, they both had sons, one named James Alan and the other named James Allan. Even their choice of pets was identical, with both men owning dogs named Toy.

Their careers and hobbies also followed parallel paths. Both Jims worked in law enforcement, one serving as a security guard and the other as a deputy sheriff. They shared a love for carpentry and mechanical drawing and even drove the same model of Chevrolet car.

In 1979, Jim Lewis decided to track down his biological family, and with the help of a local courthouse, he discovered that he had an identical twin brother. The news of their reunion made headlines, and the Jim Twins became the subject of numerous studies and documentaries as researchers sought to understand the incredible similarities between their lives.

The case fascinated psychologists and geneticists, as it provided compelling evidence for the age-old debate of nature versus nurture. Despite being raised in entirely different environments, the Jim Twins demonstrated that genetics significantly shaped their personalities, interests, and life choices.

The story of the Jim Twins serves as a powerful reminder of the mysterious forces that shape our lives. Their extraordinary tale of separation, parallel lives, and eventual reunion has captivated the world for decades, inspiring wonder and amazement. In a world filled with seemingly random events and chance encounters, the Jim Twins stand as a testament to the idea that, perhaps, some things are meant to be.

The Curse of the Iceman: A Chilling Tale of Death and Mystery

In archaeology, few discoveries have captured the public's imagination quite like that of Ötzi the Iceman. Unearthed in 1991 from the icy depths of the Italian Alps, the remarkably well-preserved mummy of a 5,300-year-old man has provided invaluable insights into the lives of our ancient ancestors. However, the story of Ötzi is not without its dark side, as a series of mysterious deaths surrounding those involved in the Iceman's discovery and research has led some to believe in a chilling curse.

The story begins on September 19, 1991, when two German hikers, Helmut and Erika Simon, stumbled upon the frozen remains of a man while traversing the Ötztal Alps. Initially, they believed the body to be that of a recently deceased mountaineer, but further investigation revealed that the mummy was, in fact, thousands of years old. The discovery of Ötzi, named after the region in which he was found, would become one of the most significant archaeological finds of the 20th century.

As researchers began to study Ötzi and unlock the secrets of his life and death, tragic events began to unfold. The first to fall victim to the alleged curse was Rainer Henn, the forensic pathologist who placed Ötzi in a body bag with his bare hands. Henn died in a car accident on his way to lecture about the Iceman. Next was Kurt Fritz, the mountain guide who led the recovery team to Ötzi's resting place. He perished in an avalanche, the only one of his party to be swept away.

The string of deaths continued with Rainer Hoelzl, the journalist who filmed the Iceman's removal from the ice, succumbing to a brain tumor. Helmut Simon, one of the hikers who discovered Ötzi, went missing during a hike in 2004, only to be found dead, having fallen more than 300 feet. Dieter Warnecke, the head of the mountain rescue team that recovered Simon's body, died of a heart attack just hours after Simon's funeral.

In total, seven people associated with the discovery and research of Ötzi have died under mysterious or tragic circumstances, leading some to believe that a curse surrounds the ancient mummy. While skeptics argue that the deaths are merely coincidental, others point to the long history of curses associated with disturbing ancient remains, such as the infamous curse of the pharaohs in Egypt.

Whether the result of a genuine curse or simply a series of unfortunate coincidences, the story of the Curse of the Iceman serves as a chilling reminder of the mysteries that still surround our ancient past. As researchers continue to study Ötzi and uncover the secrets of his life, one can only hope that the alleged curse remains a legend rather than a deadly reality.

The Lincoln-Kennedy Connection: A Tale of Eerie Parallels and Unexplained Coincidences

In the annals of American history, few figures loom as large as Abraham Lincoln and John F. Kennedy. Both presidents were known for their charisma, vision, and leadership during great national turmoil. However, beyond their political achievements, Lincoln and Kennedy share a series of uncanny coincidences that have captivated historians and conspiracy theorists alike for decades.

The Lincoln-Kennedy connection begins with the striking parallels in their political careers. Both men were elected to Congress precisely 100 years apart, with Lincoln entering the House of Representatives in 1846 and Kennedy joining the Senate in 1946. Their ascension to the presidency occurred a century apart, with Lincoln's election in 1860 and Kennedy's in 1960.

The similarities between the two presidents extend beyond their political timelines. Both men were known for their strong commitment to civil rights and faced significant opposition from the southern states. They also shared a common vision of a more united and equal America, with Lincoln's Emancipation Proclamation and Kennedy's push for civil rights legislation serving as defining moments in their respective presidencies.

However, it is the eerie connections surrounding their assassinations that have truly captured the public's imagination. Both Lincoln and Kennedy were shot in the head on a Friday while seated beside their wives. Lincoln was killed at Ford's Theatre while Kennedy was riding in a Lincoln automobile manufactured by Ford. Their assassins, John Wilkes Booth and Lee Harvey Oswald, were both Southerners who were killed before they could be brought to trial.

The coincidences do not end there. Lincoln's secretary, named Kennedy, reportedly warned him not to go to the theater on the night of his assassination, while Kennedy's secretary, named Lincoln, advised him against traveling to Dallas. After their deaths, both presidents were succeeded by vice presidents named Johnson – Andrew Johnson, who was born in 1808, and Lyndon B. Johnson, born in 1908.

Skeptics argue that many connections can be explained by mere chance or selective interpretation of historical facts. However, the sheer number of coincidences and the striking parallels between the lives and deaths of Lincoln and Kennedy continue to fuel speculation and fascination.

The Lincoln-Kennedy connection is a powerful reminder of the mysteries that still surround some of the most pivotal moments in American history. Whether the result of cosmic design or simple coincidence, the story of these two great leaders and their intertwined fates continues to captivate and intrigue, serving as a testament to the enduring power of history and the human imagination.

The Unsinkable Hugh Williams: A Maritime Tale of Survival and Serendipity

In the vast and unpredictable world of the sea, tales of shipwrecks and survival have long captured the imagination of sailors and landlubbers alike. Yet, among these stories, few are as remarkable as that of the Unsinkable Hugh Williams, a man who defied the odds not once but three times, emerging as the sole survivor of three separate shipwrecks in the treacherous waters of the Dover Strait.

The first brush with fate occurred in 1660 when a ship sailing through the Dover Strait caught itself in a violent storm. As the vessel succumbed to the raging waters, all aboard perished except for Hugh Williams. Despite the harrowing experience, Williams continued to ply his trade as a sailor, seemingly undeterred by his near-death encounter.

In 1767, more than a century later, another ship met its doom in the same waters. Once again, the vessel was claimed by the sea, and once again, a single survivor emerged from the wreckage. Astonishingly, this man also bore the name Hugh Williams. While some might dismiss this as a mere coincidence, the story of the Unsinkable Hugh Williams was far from over.

In 1820, a third ship found itself at the mercy of the unforgiving Dover Strait. As the ship sank beneath the waves, the passengers and crew faced certain death. Yet, amidst the chaos and despair, one man survived the ordeal. In a twist of fate that defies explanation, this survivor was another man named Hugh Williams.

The tale of the Unsinkable Hugh Williams has become the stuff of maritime legend, a testament to the power of chance and the resilience of the human spirit. Skeptics may argue that the story is simply an extraordinary coincidence or an embellishment of historical fact. However, for those who choose to believe, the Unsinkable Hugh Williams is a powerful reminder of the mysteries that still lurk beneath the surface of our world, waiting to be discovered and marveled at by those who dare to venture into the unknown.

The Reincarnation of Anne Frank: A Tale of Past Lives and Unexplained Memories

The story of Anne Frank, the young Jewish girl who documented her life in hiding during the Holocaust, has touched the hearts of millions worldwide. Her diary, published posthumously, stands as a testament to the resilience of the human spirit in the face of unimaginable adversity. However, the legacy of Anne Frank extends beyond her written words, as a Swedish girl named Barbro Karlen claims to be the reincarnation of the famous diarist, providing a fascinating glimpse into the world of past lives and unexplained memories.

Born in 1954, Barbro Karlen exhibited an extraordinary talent for writing from a young age. By the time she was 12, she had published several books of poetry and prose, earning her the title of a child prodigy. However, her vivid memories of her past life as Anne Frank set her apart from her peers.

Barbro's memories of her life as Anne began as a toddler. She would often speak of a previous family and a life in hiding, much to her parents' confusion. As she grew older, her memories became more detailed, and she could accurately describe the layout of the Frank family's hiding place in Amsterdam, despite never having been there before.

In 1963, Barbro and her family visited Amsterdam, and she insisted on visiting the Anne Frank House. To the astonishment of her parents and the museum staff, Barbro navigated through the building without guidance, pointing out specific details that matched Anne's descriptions in her diary. She even recognized a photograph of Anne's father, Otto Frank, and was overcome with emotion upon seeing it.

Barbro's claims of being the reincarnation of Anne Frank have been met with both fascination and skepticism. Some believe that her memories are genuine, providing evidence for past lives' existence and the soul's continuation after death. Others argue that Barbro's memories could result from an overactive imagination or exposure to Anne's story at a young age.

Regardless of one's beliefs about reincarnation, the story of Barbro Karlen and her connection to Anne Frank is a powerful reminder of the enduring impact of Anne's life and legacy. Anne Frank continues to inspire and educate generations of readers through her diary. At the same time, the tale of Barbro Karlen adds another layer of intrigue and wonder to the already extraordinary story of a young girl who refused to be silenced by the darkness of her time.

The Cab Driver Connection: A Tale of Serendipity and Literary Fate

In literature, few experiences are as magical as stumbling upon a long-sought-after book in an unexpected place. For actor Anthony Hopkins, this serendipity occurred in 1975 when he found a copy of the novel "The Girl from Petrovka" on a bench at a London train station. The discovery would lead to a series of remarkable coincidences, forever linking Hopkins to the book's author, George Feifer, in what has come to be known as the Cab Driver Connection.

Hopkins had been searching for a copy of "The Girl from Petrovka" in preparation for his role in the novel's film adaptation. Despite scouring numerous bookstores, he had been unable to find a copy. Then, as if by fate, he discovered the book lying abandoned on a bench in the train station, seemingly waiting for him to find it.

Two years later, while filming on location in Vienna, Hopkins had the opportunity to meet George Feifer, the author of "The Girl from Petrovka." During their conversation, Feifer mentioned that he had lost his personal copy of the book, which contained his annotations and notes in the margins. Intrigued, Hopkins showed Feifer the copy he had found in the train station, and to their mutual astonishment, it turned out to be the exact copy that Feifer had lost.

The Cab Driver Connection takes its name from the fact that Feifer had lent his annotated copy of the book to a friend, who had accidentally left it in the back of a London cab. The book had then made its way to the train station bench, where it was discovered by Hopkins, setting the stage for their fateful meeting in Vienna.

The story of the Cab Driver Connection serves as a powerful reminder of the mysterious forces that can shape our lives, often in ways that defy explanation. For Anthony Hopkins and George Feifer, their shared connection to "The Girl from Petrovka" created a bond that transcended the boundaries of time and space, uniting them in a tale of serendipity and literary fate that continues to captivate and inspire.

The Comet Connection: A Celestial Tale of Birth, Death, and Cosmic Coincidence

Throughout history, comets have been regarded as harbingers of change, omens of doom, and symbols of cosmic significance. For the renowned American author and humorist Mark Twain, the appearance of Halley's Comet would become inextricably linked to his life and death, creating a celestial connection that has fascinated generations of readers and stargazers alike.

Born on November 30, 1835, Mark Twain, whose real name was Samuel Langhorne Clemens, entered the world just as Halley's Comet made its closest approach to Earth. The comet, visible from Earth approximately every 75 years, has been observed and recorded by astronomers since ancient times. Its appearance has often been associated with momentous events and historical figures.

As Twain's literary career flourished, he became increasingly aware of the cosmic coincidence surrounding his birth and the appearance of Halley's Comet. In 1909, he famously predicted that he would die when the comet returned, stating, "I came in with Halley's Comet in 1835. It is coming again next year, and I expect to go out with it." Unfortunately, true to his word, Twain passed away on April 21, 1910, just one day after the comet's closest approach to Earth.

The Comet Connection between Mark Twain and Halley's Comet symbolizes the mysterious and poetic relationship between humanity and the cosmos. For Twain, the comet served as a celestial bookend to his life, marking his entrance and exit from the world in a display of cosmic synchronicity.

Skeptics may argue that Twain's prediction was simply a self-fulfilling prophecy or a mere coincidence. However, for those who choose to see the poetry in the stars, the Comet Connection is a powerful reminder of the awe-inspiring forces that govern our universe and the mysterious ways they can intersect with our lives.

Ultimately, the story of Mark Twain and Halley's Comet is a testament to the enduring power of the human imagination and our innate desire to find meaning and connection in the vast and enigmatic cosmos surrounding us.

The Hotel Time-Traveler: A Tale of Mysterious Disappearance and Temporal Intrigue

In the realm of time-travel stories and urban legends, few tales are as captivating as that of Rudolph Fentz, a man who allegedly vanished in

1876, only to reappear in the bustling streets of New York City in 1950. Dressed in 19th-century clothing and bearing items from a bygone era, Fentz's sudden appearance and subsequent death sparked a mystery that continues to fascinate and perplex those who delve into the world of temporal anomalies and unexplained phenomena.

The story begins on a summer evening in 1950 when a man dressed in Victorian-era clothing was found disoriented and confused in the middle of Times Square. Witnesses reported that the man appeared suddenly, as if out of thin air, and seemed entirely out of place amidst the modern surroundings. Before anyone could approach him, the bewildered man was struck by a car and killed.

Upon examining the man's body, police discovered several peculiar items in his pockets, including a copper token for a beer, a bill for the care of a horse, and a letter dated June 1876. Most intriguingly, the man carried identification bearing the name Rudolph Fentz.

As investigators delved into the mystery, they discovered that a man named Rudolph Fentz had indeed been reported missing in 1876, and his description matched that of the man found in Times Square. However, despite extensive efforts, no records of Fentz's life between 1876 and 1950 could be found, leading some to speculate that he had somehow traveled through time.

The Hotel Time-Traveler legend has been the subject of much debate and scrutiny, with some suggesting that the story is a work of fiction or an elaborate hoax. However, for those who entertain the possibility of time travel and the existence of temporal anomalies, the tale of Rudolph Fentz serves as a tantalizing glimpse into a world of unexplained mysteries and hidden dimensions.

Whether fact or fiction, the story of the Hotel Time-Traveler captures the imagination and invites us to ponder the nature of time, the limits of human understanding, and the tantalizing possibility that our reality may be far more complex and mysterious than we could ever imagine.

The Three Napoleon Coincidences: A Tale of Exile, Fate, and Historical Parallels

In the annals of history, few names evoke as much intrigue and fascination as Napoleon Bonaparte, the French military leader, and emperor who conquered much of Europe in the early 19th century. However, the story of Napoleon and his legacy extends beyond his military conquests. A series of uncanny coincidences connect him to two of his descendants, Napoleon III and Napoleon IV, in what has come to be known as the Three Napoleon Coincidences.

The first of these coincidences relates to how all three Napoleons met their end. Each of them died in exile on an island far from their homeland of France. Napoleon Bonaparte, the original emperor, was famously exiled to the remote island of Saint Helena in the South Atlantic after his defeat at the Battle of Waterloo. He would spend the last six years of his life on the island, ultimately dying there in 1821.

Napoleon III, the nephew of Napoleon Bonaparte, rose to power as the President of the French Second Republic and later declared himself Emperor of the French. However, his reign ended after the disastrous Franco-Prussian War, which led to his capture and subsequent exile to the island of Jersey in the English Channel. He would die there in 1873, following in the footsteps of his famous uncle.

The third and final coincidence involves Napoleon IV, the son of Napoleon III. Born in exile on the island of Saint Kitts in the Caribbean, he would never have the opportunity to rule France. Despite his efforts to reclaim the French throne, he ultimately met a tragic end, dying in a drowning accident off the coast of South Africa in 1879.

The Three Napoleon Coincidences serve as a powerful reminder of the mysterious forces that can shape history and the lives of those who play a role in it. While some may dismiss these connections as mere chance or the result of selective interpretation, others see in them a deeper pattern, a hidden hand guiding the fates of these three men who bore the name of Napoleon.

In the end, the story of the Three Napoleon Coincidences invites us to ponder the nature of fate, the cyclical patterns of history, and the enigmatic connections that can bind together the lives of those who walk the corridors of power. Whether the result of cosmic design or simple coincidence, the tale of the three Napoleons and their shared destiny continues to captivate and intrigue, serving as a testament to the enduring allure of history and the human imagination.

The Edgar Allan Poe Time Traveler: A Tale of Prophetic Fiction and Unsettling Coincidence

The works of Edgar Allan Poe, the master of the macabre, have long captivated readers with their chilling tales of mystery, horror, and suspense. However, one of his lesser-known stories, "The Narrative of Arthur Gordon Pym of Nantucket," has gained notoriety for its mysterious connection to a real-life shipwreck that occurred decades after the story's publication, leading some to speculate that Poe may have been a time traveler or possessed prophetic abilities.

Published in 1838, "The Narrative of Arthur Gordon Pym of Nantucket" tells the story of a young man who embarks on a perilous sea voyage, only to find himself and his fellow sailors stranded and facing starvation. In a desperate bid for survival, the crew draws lots to determine who will be sacrificed and cannibalized to sustain the others. The unfortunate loser of this grim lottery is a young cabin boy named Richard Parker.

In 1884, nearly 50 years after the publication of Poe's story, a real-life shipwreck occurred when the yacht Mignonette sank en route from England to Australia. The four survivors were adrift in a lifeboat with little hope of rescue and no food or water. As their situation grew increasingly dire, they made the agonizing decision to draw lots to determine who would be sacrificed for the survival of the others. In a chilling twist of fate, the cabin boy who drew the short straw was named Richard Parker, just like the character in Poe's story.

The uncanny connection between Poe's fictional tale and the real-life tragedy of the Mignonette has fueled speculation and debate among literary scholars and enthusiasts of the paranormal. Some argue that the coincidence is simply a case of life imitating art, while others suggest that Poe may have had a premonition of the future or even traveled through time to witness the events firsthand.

While the true nature of the Edgar Allan Poe Time Traveler mystery may never be fully understood, the story serves as a testament to the power of literature to blur the lines between fact and fiction and to the enduring fascination with the unknown and unexplained. In the end, the tale of Richard Parker and the mysterious connection between Poe's story and the Mignonette shipwreck invites us to ponder the mysteries of time, fate, and the human imagination and to consider the possibility that the world we inhabit may be far stranger and more wondrous than we could ever imagine.

Embracing the Mystery and Wonder of Life's Unexplained Patterns

In conclusion, the world of coincidences and synchronicities is a fascinating and mysterious realm that has captured countless individuals' imaginations throughout history. From the eerie similarities between the lives of Lincoln and Kennedy to the seemingly prophetic nature of hotels and time travel, these unexplained patterns have left us in awe and wonder.

While science and mathematics have provided some explanations for these phenomena, such as probability and chance, a sense of enchantment and curiosity remains that cannot be entirely explained. Moreover, as introduced by Carl Jung, the concept of synchronicity suggests that there may be a deeper connection between the events in our lives, one that transcends mere chance and speaks to a more profound, underlying order.

As we have seen, coincidences and synchronicities have played a significant role in developing scientific discoveries, inventions, and our personal growth and spirituality. Likewise, the power of intuition and the butterfly effect demonstrates that even the most minor events can have far-reaching consequences and that our lives are interconnected in ways that we may never fully understand.

It is crucial, however, to maintain a healthy skepticism and not fall prey to conspiracy theories or paranoia. While searching for meaning and patterns in the world around us is natural, we must also recognize that sometimes, a coincidence is just that – a coincidence.

Ultimately, the study of coincidences and synchronicities reminds us of the mystery and wonder that permeates our existence. By embracing these unexplained patterns, we open ourselves up to a deeper appreciation of life's interconnectedness and the universe's awe-inspiring complexity. In doing so, we can find a sense of purpose and meaning that transcends the mundane and allows us to see the beauty and magic beneath the surface of our everyday lives.

As we continue to explore and unravel the mysteries of our world, let us remember the power of coincidences and synchronicities to inspire, enlighten, and remind us of the infinite possibilities that life offers. In these moments of uncertainty and surprise, we are most acutely reminded of the incredible tapestry of existence and the boundless potential within each of us.

EMBRACING THE UNEXPLAINED AND
THE QUEST FOR KNOWLEDGE

As we reach the final chapter of this fascinating journey through 100 unexplained mysteries, it is important to take a moment to reflect on the significance of these enigmas and the role they play in our lives. Throughout the pages of this book, we have delved into the depths of the unknown, exploring a diverse range of mysteries that have captivated the human imagination for centuries. From the eerie legends of ghost ships and vanishing civilizations to the perplexing phenomena of crop circles and unexplained animal behavior, we have ventured into the realms of the unexplained with curiosity and wonder.

But our exploration does not end here. This book is merely a stepping stone, an invitation to venture beyond its pages and continue the quest for knowledge and understanding. The mysteries we have encountered are not simply isolated curiosities but part of a larger tapestry of human experience across cultures, time periods, and disciplines. They challenge our preconceived notions, spark our curiosity, and remind us that there is still so much to learn about the world around us.

In this concluding chapter, we will revisit some of the major themes and findings that have emerged throughout our exploration and consider the implications and significance of these unexplained mysteries in shaping our worldview. We will also acknowledge the limitations and critiques surrounding our understanding of these enigmatic phenomena and offer some final thoughts and recommendations for those wishing to continue their journey into the unknown.

As we embark on this final stage of our journey, let us remember that the pursuit of knowledge is an ongoing process and that the unexplained mysteries we have encountered serve as a testament to the boundless curiosity and resilience of the human spirit. So, let us embrace the unexplained and continue our quest for knowledge with open minds and hearts.

Unraveling the Threads of Mystery

Several overarching themes and findings emerged as we delved into the depths of the 100 unexplained mysteries presented in this book. These threads of mystery, woven together, create a tapestry that reflects the complexity and wonder of our world. In this section, we will explore these themes and discuss the insights they offer.

First and foremost, the mysteries we have examined span various disciplines and fields, from the realms of science and technology to the annals of history and the intricacies of human psychology. This diversity underscores that the unexplained is not confined to any area of study or expertise. Instead, it permeates every aspect of our lives, challenging us to question our assumptions and expand our horizons.

One of the most striking themes that emerged from our exploration is the persistence of the human desire to seek answers and make sense of the unknown. Time and again, we encountered stories of individuals who dedicated their lives to unraveling these mysteries, often at significant personal cost. This relentless pursuit of knowledge is a testament to the power of curiosity and the resilience of the human spirit.

Another key finding is the interconnectedness of these mysteries. We often discovered links and connections to other unexplained phenomena as we ventured deeper into each enigma. This interconnectedness suggests that the answers to some of these mysteries lie in understanding the broader context in which they occur and that solving one puzzle may shed light on others.

The role of perception and interpretation also emerged as a significant theme throughout our journey. Many of the mysteries we explored hinge on how we perceive and interpret the world around us, highlighting the limitations of our senses and the subjectivity of our experiences. This theme serves as a reminder that the line between the known and the unknown is often blurred and that the unexplained may sometimes be a matter of perspective.

Lastly, exploring these mysteries revealed the importance of skepticism and critical thinking in the quest for knowledge. While it is essential to approach the unexplained with an open mind, it is equally vital to scrutinize the evidence and question the conclusions that others have drawn. By doing so, we can guard against the pitfalls of dogma and superstition and ensure that our understanding of the world is grounded in reason and evidence.

In summary, our journey through the 100 unexplained mysteries has illuminated several major themes and findings, including the diversity of the unexplained, the persistence of human curiosity, the interconnectedness of mysteries, the role of perception and interpretation, and the importance of skepticism and critical thinking. These insights enrich our understanding of the mysteries themselves and offer valuable lessons for our ongoing quest for knowledge.

The Impact of the Unexplained on Our Worldview

As we examine the realm of the unexplained, it becomes increasingly apparent that these mysteries have far-reaching implications and hold great significance in shaping our understanding of the world. By exploring the unknown, we are expanding our knowledge and challenging our preconceived notions and beliefs. In this section, we will discuss the impact of the unexplained on our worldview and how these mysteries can enrich our lives.

First and foremost, the unexplained mysteries presented in this book remind us that there is still much to learn about our world and the universe beyond. In an age where information is readily available, it is easy to fall into the trap of believing that we have uncovered all there is to know. However, these mysteries act as a humbling reminder that countless phenomena still elude our understanding. Furthermore, by acknowledging the existence of the unexplained, we are prompted to adopt a more open-minded and curious approach to the world around us.

Moreover, the unexplained mysteries challenge our conventional wisdom and force us to question the validity of our current knowledge. As a result, we may find that our existing theories and explanations need to be revised or revised as we attempt to unravel these enigmas. This process of questioning and reevaluating our beliefs can lead to the development of new ideas and innovative solutions, ultimately driving the progress of human knowledge.

In addition, the unexplained can serve as a source of inspiration and wonder, sparking our imagination and fueling our creativity. The mysteries that surround us can act as a catalyst for artistic expression, scientific inquiry, and philosophical contemplation. By engaging with the unknown, we are encouraged to think beyond the boundaries of our current understanding and envision new possibilities.

Furthermore, the unexplained can profoundly affect our spirituality and connection to the universe. For some, the existence of these mysteries may provide evidence of a higher power or a divine plan, while for others, it may reinforce the belief in the interconnectedness of all things. Regardless of one's beliefs, the unexplained can remind us that there is more to our existence than meets the eye.

Finally, pursuing the unexplained can foster a sense of unity and shared purpose among individuals from diverse backgrounds and disciplines. As we collectively strive to unravel these mysteries, we are brought together by our innate curiosity and desire for knowledge. In this way, the unexplained can serve as a powerful force for collaboration and the exchange of ideas.

In conclusion, the unexplained mysteries that permeate our world have far-reaching implications and significantly shape our worldview. By embracing the unknown and embarking on the quest for knowledge, we can expand our understanding, challenge our beliefs, and enrich our lives in countless ways. As we continue our journey into the unknown, let us remember that the mysteries surrounding us are not merely obstacles to overcome but opportunities for growth, discovery, and connection.

Acknowledging the Boundaries of Our Understanding

As we explore the world of unexplained mysteries, we must recognize the limitations and critiques accompanying our quest for knowledge. While the pursuit of understanding these enigmas is undoubtedly fascinating and enriching, we must also be mindful of the boundaries within our comprehension. In this section, we will explore some key limitations and critiques that arise when attempting to unravel the threads of mystery.

First and foremost, it is crucial to acknowledge that the available evidence and information inherently limit our understanding of these unexplained mysteries. In many cases, the mysteries we have explored in this book are shrouded in uncertainty, with incomplete or conflicting data that makes it difficult to draw definitive conclusions. As such, we must be cautious in our interpretations and be open to the possibility that our current understanding may evolve as new evidence comes to light.

Another limitation we must confront is our analysis's potential for bias and subjectivity. We are prone to cognitive biases that influence our perception and interpretation of events. For instance, confirmation bias may lead us to favor information supporting our pre-existing beliefs while ignoring evidence contradicting them. In the context of unexplained mysteries, this can result in a skewed understanding that may not accurately reflect the true nature of the phenomenon in question.

Furthermore, it is essential to consider the critiques that have been leveled against the study of unexplained mysteries. Some critics argue that focusing on these enigmas distracts from more pressing and tangible issues that demand our attention, such as climate change, poverty, and social inequality. Others contend that studying unexplained mysteries is inherently unscientific, as it often relies on anecdotal evidence and subjective experiences that cannot be empirically verified.

While these critiques have merit, it is also worth noting that the study of unexplained mysteries can serve as a catalyst for scientific inquiry and innovation. By pushing the boundaries of our understanding and challenging conventional wisdom, we can inspire new lines of research and uncover groundbreaking discoveries that reshape our worldview.

In conclusion, as we acknowledge the limitations and critiques of studying unexplained mysteries, we must also recognize the value of embracing the unknown. By maintaining a healthy skepticism and a willingness to question our assumptions, we can continue to explore these enigmas with an open mind and a genuine desire for knowledge. Ultimately, through this ongoing quest for understanding, we can truly appreciate the vast and wondrous tapestry of our universe.

Continuing the Journey into the Unknown

As we reach the end of this fascinating exploration into unexplained mysteries, we must pause and reflect on our journey together. Throughout this book, we have delved into the unknown depths, seeking to understand the enigmatic phenomena that have captivated our imaginations and challenged our understanding of the world. In this final chapter, we will offer some concluding thoughts and recommendations for those who wish to continue their quest for knowledge and understanding.

The unexplained mysteries we have examined in this book are potent reminders of the vastness and complexity of our universe. From the eerie occurrences at the Bermuda Triangle to the perplexing nature of dark matter, these mysteries force us to confront the limits of our current knowledge and inspire us to push the boundaries of human understanding. As we continue to explore the unknown, we must approach these mysteries with an open mind, a healthy dose of skepticism, and a willingness to embrace the uncertainty that comes with venturing into uncharted territory.

One of the most important lessons we can take away from exploring these mysteries is the value of interdisciplinary collaboration. Many of the unexplained phenomena we have discussed in this book require the expertise of researchers from a wide range of fields, including physics, archaeology, biology, and psychology. By fostering collaboration and open communication among experts from diverse backgrounds, we can increase the likelihood of making breakthrough discoveries that shed light on these enduring enigmas.

Additionally, we must continue to invest in scientific research and education. Pursuing knowledge is a fundamental aspect of human nature, and it is through rigorous inquiry and experimentation we can unravel the mysteries that have eluded us thus far. By supporting the next generation of scientists, explorers, and thinkers, we can ensure that the quest for understanding continues long into the future.

Finally, we must remember that the discovery process is often as important as the discoveries themselves. The unexplained mysteries we have explored in this book serve as powerful catalysts for curiosity, wonder, and critical thinking. As we continue to seek answers to these enigmatic questions, we must also embrace the journey itself, for we grow as individuals and as a society through this process of inquiry and exploration.

In conclusion, the world of unexplained mysteries is vast, complex, and endlessly fascinating. As we close the pages of this book, we encourage you to continue your journey into the unknown, armed with curiosity, skepticism, and a sense of wonder. Remember that the quest for knowledge is a lifelong endeavor and that the mysteries we have explored here are a small sample of the countless enigmas awaiting discovery. So, keep asking questions, seeking answers, and never stop exploring the uncharted territories of our universe.

ABOUT THE AUTHOR

Luke Marsh, a passionate philosopher and critical thinker, has now ventured into the realm of trivia and fascinating facts with his latest series, "The Ultimate 100 Series". Known for his deep love for exploring the complexities of the world, Luke has spent years delving into the depths of philosophical thought, which has now translated into a series that explores the most intriguing, bizarre, and awe-inspiring aspects of our world. Each book in this exhilarating series is a testament to Luke's curiosity and knack for uncovering the extraordinary in the ordinary. When he's not writing or thinking deeply, Luke can be found outdoors, spending time with loved ones, or lost in a good book. With "The Ultimate 100 Series", Luke invites you to join him on a rollercoaster ride of discovery, perfect for trivia buffs, curious minds, and adventure seekers alike.

$10.99 ~~FREE EBOOK~~

Receive Your Free Copy of 100+ Interesting Real Stories

Or visit:
bookboundstudios.wixsite.com/luke-marsh

Printed in Great Britain
by Amazon